INTERNATIONAL JUSTICE FOR FORME

NIJHOFF LAW SPECIALS

VOLUME 20

The titles published in this series are listed at the end of this volume.

INTERNATIONAL JUSTICE FOR FORMER YUGOSLAVIA

The Working of the
International Criminal Tribunal of the Hague

by

Karine Lescure and Florence Trintignac

KLUWER LAW INTERNATIONAL
THE HAGUE / LONDON / BOSTON

A C.I.P. Catalogue record for this book is available from the Library of Congress.

ISBN 90-411-0201-9

Published by Kluwer Law International,
P.O. Box 85889, 2508 CN The Hague, The Netherlands.

Sold and distributed in the U.S.A. and Canada
by Kluwer Law International,
675 Massachusetts Avenue, Cambridge, MA 02139, U.S.A.

In all other countries, sold and distributed
by Kluwer Law International,
P.O. Box 85889, 2508 CN The Hague, The Netherlands.

Printed on acid-free paper

Printed in the Netherlands

THE SCIENTIFIC COMMITTEE

Antoine **BERNARD (FIDH)**
Françoise **BOUCHET-SAULNIER (MSF)**
William **BOURDON (FIDH)**
Brigitte **STERN (CEDIN-PARIS I)**

THE AUTHORS:

Karine **LESCURE:**
Jurist, author of a previous work entitled "Le
Tribunal pénal international pour l'ex-
Yougoslavie" [An International Criminal
Tribunal for Former Yugoslavia]
published by Editions Montchrestien.

Florence **TRINTIGNAC:** Ph.D. in Political
Science at the IEP in Paris.

"It is particularly striking to observe to what extent the victims hope that the Commission will establish the truth and that the international Tribunal will ensure that justice prevails. All the parties expect it. One is thus forced to conclude that the future demands justice and that justice begins by establishing the truth. The Commission would be failing in its duty if it did not emphasize the hopes of the victims, the intergovernmental organisations, the non-governmental organisations, the media and world public opinion. Consequently, the international Tribunal needs to have available the necessary resources and support to enable it to live up to these hopes and do its job well., Furthermore, since the nations are expecting a new world order based on international public order, there is a need to establish permanent and effective bodies to dispense international justice. The international war crimes Tribunal for former Yugoslavia should thus lead the way in this direction".

Extract from the final report of the Commission of Experts set up under the terms of Resolution 780 (1992) of the Security Council.

TABLE OF CONTENTS

PREFACES   xi

INTRODUCTION   1

I.
GENERAL PRESENTATION OF THE TRIBUNAL AND
ITS OPERATION   11

I.   ORGANISATION OF THE COURT   13

II.   JURISDICTION OF THE TRIBUNAL   17
        1.   Jurisdiction *ratione loci*   17
        2.   Jurisdiction *ratione temporis*   17
        3.   Jurisdiction *ratione materiae:* punishable crimes   19
        4.   *ratione personae* Jurisdiction: the guilty parties 29

III.   PROCEDURES   33

II.
AID, PROTECTION AND FACILITIES AVAILABLE TO
VICTIMS AND WITNESSES   37

I.   FINANCIAL AND INSTITUTIONAL ASPECTS
        OF AID AND PROTECTION   39
        1.   The need for an adequate budget   39
        2.   The distribution of aid to victims and witnesses   40

II.   PROTECTION GIVEN TO VICTIMS AND WITNESSES:
        INDISPENSABLE BUT STILL INADEQUATE   43
        1.   Explicit and direct protection: the inadequacies   45
        2.   Explicit but indirect protection   47
        3.   The question of protection of victims and witnesses
             from national jurisdictions   49

III.   LIGHTENING THE BURDEN OF PROOF:
        THE EXAMPLE OF SEXUAL ASSAULT   51

III.
THE CRUX OF THE MATTER: TRYING THE CRIMINALS   59

I.   TRYING THE CRIMINALS: COOPERATION FROM
STATES IS A NECESSITY   61
1.   The apportionment of jurisdictions between the
Tribunal and the National Jurisdictions   62
2.   Cooperation from the states and legal aid   70

II.   TRYING THE CRIMINALS: THE RESOURCES
ALLOCATED   81
1.   Remanding the accused to the custody of the court   81
2.   Absence of the accused: an obstacle to prosecution
and conviction: 85
3.   A penal responsibility that would be difficult to
dispute   88

CONCLUSION   91

SUMMARY BIBLIOGRAPHY   99

ORGANIZATIONS WHICH TOOK THE INITIATIVE
TO PRODUCE THIS BOOK   105

APPENDICES   111

-    Security Council Resolution 808 (22 February, 1993)
-    Security Council Resolution 827 (25 May, 1993)
-    Rules of procedure and evidence of the Hague
Tribunal (as amended 6 October 1995)

PREFACES

On 25 May, 1993 the United Nations Organisation, representing the international community as a whole, instituted an international criminal court for former Yugoslavia. This was a major event for all those who are concerned about the virtual suppression – despite declarations of principle – of serious breaches of international humanitarian law and the introduction of laws designed to protect human rights. It was an event of great symbolic significance, even though the obvious ambiguities in its creation should not be overlooked.

CEDIN, the Centre de Droit International, an institution devoted to academic research, has always been aware of current events, according priority to dialogue with practitioners and concerned with the promotion of the rule of law in international society.

In its awareness of current events, CEDIN has allotted itself the task of objectively analysing international incidents, so as to provide those playing a leading role in international affairs with a frame of reference to help them come to the right decisions.

In its relationship with practitioners, CEDIN warmly welcomed the cooperation between two non-governmental organisations, one the FIDH, oriented towards the protection of human rights and the other, the MSF, more concerned with the concrete implementation of humanitarian law. This collaboration between theoretical considerations and experience in the field on the one hand and a university institution and NGOs for the protection of human rights and humanitarian law on the other showed itself to be extremely fruitful as work on this book progressed.

However, this approach, which focuses on reality and practice, only makes sense in relation to its purpose, namely, the promotion of respect for international law especially in the field of human rights. International relations are known to oscillate constantly between law and aggression. It is also clear that any progress in international law causes a corresponding retreat of violence in international relations. This objective is particularly important in the realm of international criminal law which has for so long remained in its embryonic stage.

Everything is now converging to make the work of the International Law Commission more of a reality, placing the creation of a permanent International Criminal Court on the agenda as well as the creation of a criminal court for former Yugoslavia.

This book aims at participating in this movement, by presenting both a critical analysis of this new institution and instructions for the benefit of all those who are involved, in order to encourage maximum use of this Tribunal.

The fate of a future permanent international criminal court, designed to punish the most odious crimes, depends on the failure or the – hoped-for – success of this Tribunal.

Brigitte STERN
Director of CEDIN Paris I

The Rwandan genocide has reminded us of the imperative for justice which had so recently appealed to every individual confronted with the tragedies of former Yugoslavia.

The imperative for justice is the whole reason for the demand which the FIDH has been making for the past 70 years for a permanent international criminal court to bring to justice the perpetrators of serious breaches of human rights where national justice fails to do so, thus stopping history from repeating itself.

Thanks to the creation of an international criminal Tribunal for former Yugoslavia, a unique first step has been taken in this direction. What is more, unlike the Nuremberg and Tokyo Tribunals, this was not a Tribunal of the victors but a Tribunal of the whole international community.

The mobilisation of public opinion certainly played a part in favour of the swift creation of this jurisdiction. However, its effective operation was dependent upon the willingness of countries to cooperate with it. On this point, if only on a strictly budgetary level, serious doubts have been expressed, to say nothing of the risk of a paralysis in judicial cooperation, without which the Tribunal would lose all its effectiveness.

It is therefore vital for public opinion to remain mobilized. That is the reason for this book, the result of a multi-disciplinary and unique alliance between an NGO for the defence of human rights, the International Federation of Leagues of Human Rights

(FIDH) a humanitarian NGO, Médecins sans Frontières (MSF) and CEDIN, an international law research centre.

As well as being a tool for the practitioner this guide also aims to enable every citizen to understand the workings of the international justice rendered in his or her name and to make his or her voice heard so that such justice shall be rendered effectively.

Daniel JACOBY
President of the FIDH

In 1992, Médecins sans Frontières published its first report on ethnic cleansing in Bosnia. In June, 1994, MSF sent the United Nations its first report on genocide in Rwanda. Between these two events there lies the road trodden by a humanitarian medical organisation increasingly constrained to highlight the areas in which it operates in order to reach those it is trying to help.

MSF has chosen to put names to the crimes, to restore the victims' identity and dignity, so that the cloak of assistance shall not be used to conceal the instigator of the tragedy and confuse it with its victim. That is because the effects of an earthquake and those of genocide cannot be treated in the same way, except in an effort to arouse compassion and human solidarity.

There is an ongoing debate, however, between those who believe that humanitarianism should treat and alleviate suffering without preoccupying itself with the causes of evil and those who believe that the act of assistance is not the sum total of the act of humanity. It is becoming easier and easier to confuse impartiality with blindness. The humanitarian principle of impartiality consists in offering help to the victims without discrimination as to political, ethnic or religious affiliation. In short, it requires the carer to help any individual as soon as he or she becomes a victim, and to remain blind to political, military and financial exploitation of the victims by those who are continuing their struggle for power. Each individual involved in humanitarian action has a duty to denounce what any humanitarian law would define as breach of trust, namely, the misuse of humanitarian aid by channelling into military objectives.

Humanitarian law is not dogmatic law. It has always held the front line between aggression and survival. It thus integrates, by its very nature, political and military contingencies. The difficult relationship between the just and the good, the just and the unjust, is tackled clearly and without heroic ambiguity. This law imposes clear commitments of justice which are binding upon every country. In this philosophy of least harm which underlies humanitarian law, justice does not emerge as a luxury but as a vital landmark to avoid folly, an essential buttress to stop the syndrome of violence generating violence. This law provides for the commitment of every country to seek out and try war criminals, even in the absence of an international Tribunal. The international justice nascent before the Hague Tribunal cannot develop in the face of cowardice by the courts of the nations.

The creation of an international criminal court for former Yugoslavia is the culmination of a process of hypocrisy and idealism, of cowardice and heroic obstinacy. The risks for the victims and all the imperfections of this Tribunal ought not to be allowed to conceal the formidable revolution constituted by the current debate concerning international criminal justice. Having attempted to maintain peace to the detriment of justice, the international community is talking of rendering justice to re-establish peace. By so doing, it is toppling the myth of the impunity of the victors. The Tribunal will attempt to combat force by using an unconventional weapon which within the closed field of its precincts will bring those who have nothing left to lose face to face with those who have everything to gain.

Médecins sans Frontières decided to back this initiative in order to remain by the sides of the victims in this new episode of their drama to be enacted before the international Tribunal. This book hopes to explain what is involved, the strengths and weaknesses of this institution, to explain in detail the complexities of its procedures in order to help the victims and witnesses to make their choice in the light of the risks involved and the foreseeable results.

It also hopes to appeal to the non-governmental organizations, offering them an instrument whereby they can invoke humanitarian law without betraying it, and implement it by serving the weakest.

Philippe BIBERSON
President of MEDECINS SANS FRONTIERES

INTRODUCTION

While the conflict was still raging in former Yugoslavia and peace negotiations continued to be fruitless, the United Nations decided to create an international body to try war criminals directly implicated in the most basic human rights breaches which have typified the conflict in former Yugoslavia since its inception.

In 1993, the Security Council resolved, in the name of the international community, through its resolutions 808 and 827, to create *"an international Tribunal with the sole purpose of judging those persons deemed responsible for serious human rights breaches committed on the territory of former Yugoslavia since 1991 (...) and to adapt the Statute of International Tribunal to this end"*.

The context in which this resolution was passed is one of the special features of this Tribunal. The process of the ad hoc creation of an international organ of justice competent to try war criminals in the name of the international community while the adversaries were still confronting each other is fundamentally different from that established by the Nuremberg Tribunal. The latter was initiated as the result of a decision taken by the victorious States in World War II, once hostilities had ended.

In the case of the Tribunal for former Yugoslavia, the community of nations, through the Security Council, the main restraining body of the United Nations Organisation (UNO) was behind its creation, which provides it with both eminently international and political credentials. This international dimension will certainly enable the Tribunal and its members not to be exposed to the criticism expressed concerning the Nuremberg Tribunal according to which the justice then rendered was that of the victors.

By creating this Tribunal in time of war, the Security Council created this body as an instrument in the peace process and thus conferred upon it a political dimension the management of which constitutes one of the most important factors for those who are responsible for ensuring its operation. *The deployment of law in the cause of peace* is certainly a most significant innovation in the creation of such a Tribunal. It is the result of several demands which weighed and continue to weigh upon the conscience of the international community in the context of the conflict in former Yugoslavia.

The political requirement is the prime consideration. It would be impossible to devise a peace plan acceptable to all the protagonists, since the multitude of torments inflicted upon civilian populations, ethnic cleansing and the massive rapes that have occurred in its wake, displacements of populations and prisoner camps, all extensively described in the media, have caused numerous outcries in public opinion. It is this pressure which is gradually making the taking of concrete steps indispensable.

The moral requirement is also closely linked to the political requirement. There is a moral requirement to establish an international and impartial form of justice to combat the immunity from prosecution of those responsible for the tortures and breaches of humanitarian international law. Herein lies the real aim of the international criminal Tribunal for former Yugoslavia. It is to try war criminals in complete independence whatever their place in the civil or military hierarchy and their community of origin, whether Serb, Croat or Bosnian Moslem. It is this same moral requirement that legitimises the decision to establish this Tribunal even while the battles continue to rage in the territory which was once Yugoslavia. The Tribunal is, in fact, being called upon to play a deterrent role in relation to the various parties to the conflict by introducing the idea that the commanders and political leaders will have to answer for their actions before an international court of law.

The legal requirement, one which is linked to the gradual emergence of a feeling of responsibility among the international community as regards the protection and defence of human rights. This process is based on the creation of a number of laws, conventions and international decrees which are the result of an important process of standardisation, developed mainly after World War II. The development of the legal protection of human rights contributed to the development of international humanitarian law and the emergence of the concept of international criminal responsibility of individuals in cases of serious breach of humanitarian law. Humanitarian law can be defined as the whole array *"of principles and rules which limit recourse to violence during a period of armed conflict"*.[1] It was aimed at *"protecting those persons which are not or are no longer directly engaged in hostilities – the wounded, shipwrecked prisoners of war and civilians; [and to] limit the effects of violence in combat to attain the objectives of the conflict"*.[2] Humanitarian international law is thus shown to concern the protection of the rights of man in the specific context of armed conflicts. It is accepted that in times of war or in cases of exceptional public danger, certain human rights may be restricted under special circumstances. It is in relation to serious breaches of humanitarian international law, however, that the international Tribunal for former Yugoslavia has to formulate its judgements.

---

1.   UNITED NATIONS. International Humanitarian Law and the Rights of Man, Information Sheet No. 13, Geneva, United Nations, May 1992, p.1.
2.   *Ibid.*

It is on the basis of these three requirements, political, moral and legal, that the process started for the creation of an international Tribunal for former Yugoslavia, a process which was also constrained by the imperative of speed. The international community had a duty to create the instruments vital to the inauguration and operation of such a Tribunal and to do so as quickly as possible. This imperative explains the uniqueness and the innovative nature of the procedure which enabled the UN to grant the Tribunal its existence and above all legal and political legitimacy. The interpretation thus given to Chapter VII of the Charter, used as the legal framework, requires some clarification.

Chapter VII establishes the principle of the Security Council's main responsibility to maintain and re-establish international peace and security and to this end confers specific prerogatives upon it. In affirming that the situation generated by the virtually systematic breaches of international humanitarian law in former Yugoslavia constituted a threat to international peace and security under the terms of Article 39 of Chapter VII, the Security Council provided itself with the means to apply Article 41 of the same chapter. This article enables it, in such a situation, to take adequate **measures not involving the use of armed force**. The measures actually quoted are of an economic nature (complete or partial rupture of economic ties and rail, sea and air links, etc.), but this is not exclusively the case because Article 41 also envisages the breaking of diplomatic relations.

Although the creation of a criminal jurisdiction may seem very far removed from such measures, the formulation of the second sentence in Article 41 *"these may include"* clearly shows the exemplary and non-restrictive nature of the list, thus leaving it open to the Council to conceive of other measures not involving armed force, on condition, however, that they prove to be **necessary.**

The Security Council has thus made an effort to prove the existence of this necessity to justify its action as witnessed by resolutions 808 and 827. According to the Council, the creation of

CHARTER OF THE UNITED NATIONS
CHAPTER I
PURPOSES AND PRINCIPLES
Article 2

The Organization and its Members, in pursuit of the Purposes stated in Article 1, shall act in accordance with the following Principles.

1. The Organization is based on the principle of the sovereign equality of all its Members.

2. All Members, in order to ensure to all of them the rights and benefits resulting from membership, shall fulfil in good faith the obligations assumed by them in accordance with the present Charter.

3. All Members shall settle their international disputes by peaceful means in such a manner that international peace and security, and justice, are not endangered.

4. All Members shall refrain in their international relations from the threat or use of force against the territorial integrity or political independence of any state, or in any other manner inconsistent with the Purposes of the United Nations.

CHAPTER VII
ACTION WITH RESPECT TO THREATS TO THE PEACE, BREACHES OF THE PEACE, AND ACTS OF AGGRESSION
Article 39

The Security Council shall determine the existence of any threat to the peace, breach of the peace, or act of aggression and shall make recommendations, or decide what measures shall be taken in accordance with Articles 41 and 42, to maintain or restore international peace and security.

Article 40

In order to prevent an aggravation of the situation, the Security Council may, before making the recommendations or deciding upon the measures provided for in Article 39, call upon the parties concerned to comply with such provisional measures as it deems necessary or desirable. Such provisional measures shall be without prejudice to the rights, claims, or position of the parties concerned. The Security Council shall duly take account of failure to comply with such provisional measures.

Article 41

The Security Council may decide what measures not involving the use of armed force are to be employed to give effect to its decisions, and it may call upon the Members of the United Nations to apply such measures. These may include complete or partial interruption of economic relations and of rail, sea, air, postal, telegraphic, radio, and other means of communication, and the severance of diplomatic relations.

Article 42

Should the Security Council consider that measures provided for in Article 41 would be inadequate or have proved to be inadequate, it may take such action by air, sea, or land forces as may be necessary to maintain or restore international peace and security. Such action may include demonstrations, blockade, and other operations by air, sea, or land forces of Members of the United Nations.

a court has emerged as an appropriate measure because under the current circumstances it is of such a nature as to achieve or facilitate the goal of re-establishing international peace and security in the territory of former Yugoslavia.

The Security Council thus confirms in these two texts that the Tribunal would **act as a deterrent** thereby enabling or facilitating the re-establishment of international peace and security, and thus integrating it as fully as possible into the process of re-establishing peace in the territory of former Yugoslavia.

This poses a problem for the current trend to question the terms of reference of the Security Council. The original interpretation of the system in Chapter VII of the Charter did not confer upon the Security Council, as a political organ, the task of dispensing international justice nor to pose as the defender of the international rule of law. However, if such a question is to constitute a topic for consideration for jurists, the emergency situation which prevailed and which still prevails in former Yugoslavia explains and above all legitimates the choice of the Security Council as the instrument. Only by resorting to Chapter VII would it be possible to guarantee swift reaction.

These political and legal conditions and above all the urgent need to create the Tribunal have had their effect on the nature of the instruments with which the Tribunal has been equipped for its operation. The judges have devised Regulations designed to establish the rules of internal procedure. The desired and indispensable cohabitation of the representatives of various legal systems in effect throughout the world, the need for speed to initiate the first bills of indictment and open the first cases may sometimes lead to a belief that "law has been made with the impossible" and that in this instance the law is the result of a political and legal compromise. These questions certainly still remain unanswered. Problems have arisen and will certainly emerge as and when proceedings are launched, such as the difficult balance to be achieved between the rights of the defence and the protection of victims and witnesses. The groundwork already laid by the judges and various commissions of inquiry as well as the good will of certain non-governmental organisations (NGOs) make it possible to hope the objective of fighting immunity from punishment determined in a court of law to achieve.

This book is designed to contribute to the process by calling upon the decision-makers involved to make their contribution to the Tribunal both on a political and a material level and to explain its workings to world leaders as well as members of NGOs, journalists, lawyers and so on, so that they may assist those victims who want to apprise the Tribunal of their plight and testify to it, an essential requirement for bringing those responsible to justice.

I.
GENERAL PRESENTATION OF THE TRIBUNAL AND ITS OPERATION

The Tribunal to be established in the case of former Yugoslavia has a duty to an even greater extent, if possible, than the criminal courts of any democratic state, to respect the fundamental rights of the individual and especially the right to a defence. This is due, of course, to the exemplary nature conferred by the international dimension of the cases to be heard.

I. ORGANISATION OF THE COURT

- **Note concerning the qualification and election of judges**

Under **Article 13 of the Statute of the International Court of Justice**, *"The Court shall be composed of a body of independent judges, elected regardless of their nationality from among persons of high moral character, who possess the qualifications required in their respective countries for appointment to the highest judicial offices, or are jurisconsults of recognised competence in international law"*. Members of the United Nations and non-member States which maintain permanent observers at the headquarters of the Organisation are entitled to submit candidates for office to the Secretary-General and these are then forwarded to the Security Council.

CURRENT COMPOSITION OF THE TRIBUNAL
Presiding judge of the Tribunal and the court of appeal
• Antonio Cassese (Italy)

Members of the Court of Appeal
• Georges Abi-Saab (Egypt)
• Jules Deschenes (Canada)
• Haopei Li (China)
• Sir Ninian Stephen (Australia)

Presiding judges of each of the two lower courts
• Gabrielle Kirk McDonald (United States)
• Adolphus Godwin-Karibi-Whyte (Nigeria)

Judges of the two lower courts
• Rustam S. Sidhwa (Pakistan)
• Lal Chand Vohrah (Malaysia)
• Claude Jorda (France), successor to G. Le Foyer de Costil who resigned for medical reasons.
• Elisabeth Odio Benito (Costa Rica)
    Vice-Chair of the Tribunal

"On the basis of these candidacies, the Council shall draw up a list of a minimum of 22 candidates and a maximum of 33 candidates, duly taking account of the need to ensure adequate representation for the world's main legal systems". The list is submitted to the General Assembly which elects 11 judges for a four-year renewable term of office.

The presence of judges of various nationality demonstrates the desire of the General Assembly to ensure that the various legal systems in force throughout the world are properly represented. However, the clear predominance of representatives of the common law system is notable (8 judges). Furthermore, only two judges represent European countries sit when the hearing involves a conflict on that continent. None are from central or eastern Europe. The lack of equal representation between the two sexes is also noteworthy.

This diversity explains some of the difficulties which the judges have encountered when compiling the rules of the court in order to reach a compromise in law on certain points.

- **Note concerning the appointment of the Prosecutor**

The Prosecutor is appointed by the Security Council at the recommendation of the Secretary-General.

Prosecutor:
Richard Goldstone (South Africa)
(a common law country)

Deputy prosecutor:
Graham Blewitt (Australia, a common law country)

There has been a call for the appointment of a second deputy prosecutor, this time from a civil law country.

In order to make it possible to better understand the organization of the Tribunal, we consider it best to present it in the form of a diagram. This should make it much clearer. The diagram is to be found at the end of this book.

II. JURISDICTION OF THE TRIBUNAL

1. JURISDICTION *RATIONE LOCI*

The Tribunal only has jurisdiction over crimes committed in the territory of former Yugoslavia which represents the former Socialist Federal Republic of Yugoslavia, consisting of the land space, air space and territorial waters. This geographical limitation on jurisdiction is linked to the legal basis on which the court was created and which is based exclusively on a resolution passed by the Security Council under Chapter VII of the United Nations Charter (resolution 827), a resolution which itself applies only to the territory of former Yugoslavia. Since the Tribunal is only a "subsidiary organ" of the Security Council (Article 29 of the Charter), it cannot be equipped with a geographical competence not possessed by the body from which it emanates.

2. JURISDICTION *RATIONE TEMPORIS*

The court only has jurisdiction concerning crimes committed after 1 January, 1991, which according to the Security Council is the date which marks the outbreak of hostilities in the territory of former Yugoslavia. Here again, the restriction of jurisdiction is based on Chapter VII of the United Nations Charter, since the

BASIS FOR THE JURISDICTION OF THE TRIBUNAL

The Tribunal has jurisdiction by virtue of customary international humanitarian law, as formulated in the following official conventions:

- THE GENEVA CONVENTIONS OF 12 AUGUST 1949

- THE FOURTH HAGUE CONVENTION OF 18 OCTOBER 1907

- THE CONVENTION ON GENOCIDE OF 9 DECEMBER 1948

- THE STATUTE OF THE NUREMBERG MILITARY TRIBUNAL OF 8 AUGUST 1945

Security Council is only empowered to create this jurisdiction with the purpose of re-establishing peace.

3. JURISDICTION *RATIONE MATERIAE*: PUNISHABLE CRIMES

Under the Statute, the law applicable by the Tribunal is based on rules of conventional and customary law. In the opinion of the Secretary-General, *"the principle of nummum crimen sine lege requires the international Tribunal to apply the rules of international humanitarian law which are, without a doubt, part of customary law in such a way that the problem arising from the fact that certain States, though not all, are signatories to specific conventions, is not applicable"*. Furthermore, it is vital that the activities which are to be punished afflict the conscience of the entire international community.

According to the Statute, *"That part of international humanitarian law which has indisputably become customary international law is the law applicable to armed conflict, namely: the Geneva Conventions of 12 August, 1949, the Fourth Hague Convention and the rules concerning the laws and conventions of war on land of 1907, the Convention of 9 December, 1948 for the prevention and suppression of the crime of genocide and the Statute of the Military Tribunal of Nuremberg of 8 August, 1945"*.

- **The Geneva Conventions and serious human rights breaches**

The Geneva Conventions lay down the rules of international humanitarian law and stipulate the basic rules of customary law applicable in international armed conflicts. They govern the conduct of war from a humanitarian point of view by protecting certain categories of people.

INTERNATIONAL GENEVA CONVENTIONS
of 1949 consists of:

- **CONVENTION NO. 1 to improve the lot of the wounded and sick in the armed forces during a campaign**

- **CONVENTION NO. 2 to improve the lot of the wounded, sick and shipwrecked in armed conflict at sea**

- **CONVENTION NO. 3 concerning the treatment of prisoners of war**

- **CONVENTION NO. 4 concerning the protection of civilians in wartime**

Serious breaches of the Geneva Convention feature under **Article 50 of Convention No. 1**, under **Article 51 of Convention No. 2, Article 130 of Convention No. 3** and in **Article 147 of Convention No. 4**, as well as in **Article 3,** which is common to the four Geneva Conventions and which state the minimum rules applicable in case of internal armed conflict.

Under the terms of Article 2 of the Statute of the Tribunal, which repeats the definition of the Geneva Conventions, these serious breaches are: intentional homicide, torture or inhuman treatment, including biological experiments, the act of intentionally causing great suffering or to seriously damage physical integrity or health, the destruction and appropriation of property which is not justified militarily and performed on a grand scale illegally and arbitrarily, the act of forcing a prisoner of war

ARTICLE 3 — CONFLICTS OF A NON-INTERNATIONAL NATURE*

In the case of an armed conflict of a non-international nature arising on the territory of one of the above contracting Parties, each of the Parties to the conflict shall be required to apply at least the following provisions:

1) Those persons not participating directly in the hostilities, including those forces of the armed forces who have laid down their arms and those persons who have been put out of action by illness, injury, imprisonment or for any other reason shall be treated humanely under all circumstances, without any unfavourable discrimination being made on the grounds of race, colour, religion or belief, sex, birth, wealth or any similar criteria.

To this end, the following are shall remain prohibited, at any time and in any place, in relation to the persons abovementioned:

a) Attempts to take life or harm any part of the body, especially murder in all its forms, mutilation, cruel treatment, torture and torment;

b) The taking of hostages;

c) Treatment likely to affect human dignity, especially humiliating and degrading treatment;

d) Sentencing pronounced and executions performed without a prior judgement delivered by a regularly constituted court, furnished with the judicial guarantees recognised as indispensable among civilised nations.

2) The wounded and the sick shall be accepted and treated.

An impartial humanitarian body, such as the International Committee of the Red Cross, may offer its services to the Parties to the conflict.

The Parties to the conflict shall further attempt, by means of special agreements, all or part of the other terms of this Convention.

The application of the above provisions shall not affect the legal status of the Parties to the conflict.

ARTICLE 147 — SERIOUS BREACHES

The serious breaches mentioned in the previous article are those which involve one or more of the following actions if they are committed against persons or property protected by the Convention: intentional homicide, torture or inhuman treatment, including biological experiments, the act of intentionally causing serious suffering or to seriously affecting physical integrity or health, deportation or illegal transfer, illegal detention, the act of forcing a protected person to serve in the armed forces of the enemy Power, or that of depriving him or her of his or her right to be judged regularly and impartially under the terms of the present Convention, the taking of hostages, the destruction and appropriation of property which is militarily unjustified and performed on a large scale, illicitly and arbitrarily.

---

* Article common to all four Covenants

or a civilian to serve in the armed forces of the enemy power, the act of depriving a prisoner of war or a civilian of his or her right to be judged normally and impartially, the expulsion or illegal transfer of a civilian or his or her illegal detention and the taking of civilians as hostages.

- **The Hague Convention of 1907 (IV) and breaches of laws or customs of war on land**

The Hague Convention constitutes an important area of customary international humanitarian law which is currently part of customary international law. The rules of the Hague Convention apply to aspects of customary international law, as do the Geneva Conventions of 1949. But they go further in recognising that the right of belligerents to wage war is not unlimited (**Article 22**) and that recourse to certain methods is prohibited by the rules of war on land (**Article 23**).

Under the terms of **Article 3** of the Statute of the Tribunal, breaches of laws or conventions of war include, but are not restricted to, the use of toxic weapons or other weapons designed to cause unnecessary suffering, the groundless destruction of towns and villages or the devastation that is not militarily justified, attack or bombing by any means of undefended towns, villages, human habitations or buildings, the seizure, destruction or deliberate damage to buildings devoted to religious purposes, to welfare or to teaching, to the arts and sciences, historical monuments, works of art and works of a scientific nature and looting of public or private property.

Fourth Hague Convention, 1907

SECTION II — HOSTILITIES

CHAPTER I — Methods of attacking the enemy, sieges and bombing

ARTICLE 22
The belligerents shall not have the unlimited right of choice of methods they use to attack the enemy.

ARTICLE 23
Apart from the prohibitions covered by special agreements, the following are especially prohibited:

a) The use of poison or poisoned weapons;

b) Killing or wounding through the betrayal of individuals from the enemy nation or army;

c) Killing or wounding an enemy who, having laid down his or her arms or no longer able to defend himself or herself, has surrendered;

d) To declare that no quarter shall be given;

e) To use arms, projectiles or materials designed to cause unnecessary harm;

f) To misuse the parliamentary flag, the national flag or the military insignia and uniform of the enemy, as well as the distinctive marks of the Geneva Convention;

g) To destroy or to seize enemy property, except in cases where such destruction or seizure are necessary for the prosecution of the war;

h) To declare that the national rights of the other Party are abolished, suspended or unrecognised in law;

It is also forbidden to a belligerent to force nationals of the opposing Party to take part in military operations directed against their country, even if they have been in its service prior to the start of the war.

ARTICLE 24
Military ploys and the use of the resources required to discover intelligence about the enemy and on the ground are considered to be legitimate.

ARTICLE 25
It is forbidden to attack or bomb, by any means whatsoever, towns, villages, human habitations or buildings which are undefended.

ARTICLE 26
The commander of the attacking forces, before commencing the bombing, and except in the case of a heavy attack, must do everything he can to warn the authorities.

ARTICLE 27
In sieges or bombings, every possible measures must be taken to spare, as far as possible, buildings dedicated to worship, the arts, the sciences and social welfare, historic monuments, hospitals and places where the sick and wounded are assembled, on condition that these are not also used for military purposes.

It is the duty of the besieged to designate such buildings or places of assembly using special, visible signs which shall be notified in advance to the besiegers.

ARTICLE 28
It is forbidden to allow looting of a town or locality captured in an attack

- **The 1948 Convention and the customary law relating to genocide**

Genocide is a punishable crime, whether committed in peacetime or in wartime. This prohibition which applies to every state whether or not it has ratified the 1948 Convention on the subject, as is shown in the consultative opinion of the International Court of Justice dated 28 May, 1951 concerning the question of exceptions to the said Convention. *"The principles behind the Convention are principles which are acknowledged by civilised nations as binding upon States, regardless of any separate agreement"*. The 1948 Convention on Genocide has become part of customary international law.

The Statute of the Tribunal, **reproduces Articles 2 and 3 in their entirety**. Under the terms of these articles, genocide covers any of the following act committed with the intention of destroying, entirely or partially, a national, ethnic, racial or religious group, such as: murder of members of the group; serious attack on the physical or mental integrity of members of the group; intentional submission of the group to conditions of existence which are designed to cause its complete or partial physical annihilation; measures designed to prevent births within the group; forced transfer of children in the group to another group. The following acts are punishable: genocide, conspiracy to commit genocide, attempted genocide and complicity in genocide **(Article 4 of the Statute)**.

CONVENTION FOR THE PREVENTION AND REPRESSION OF THE CRIME OF GENOCIDE

ARTICLE 2

Under the present Convention, genocide is covered by one of the following acts committed with intent to destroy, in whole or in part, any national, ethnic, racial or religious group such as:

a) Murder of members of the group;
b) Serious physical or mental damage to members of the group;
c) Intentional submission of the group to conditions of existence which are liable to cause its total or partial physical destruction;
d) Measures designed to prevent births within the group;
e) Forcible transfer of children from the group to another group.

ARTICLE 3

The following acts are punishable:

a) Genocide;
b) Conspiracy to commit genocide;
c) Direct and public incitement to commit genocide;
d) Attempted genocide;
e) Complicity in genocide.

ARTICLE 4

Those persons who have committed genocide or any of the other acts listed under Article 3 shall be punished, whether they are rulers, officials or individuals.

ARTICLE 9

Disputes between the signatory Parties as regards the interpretation, application or performance of the present Convention, including those concerning the responsibility of a State in the matter of genocide or any of the other acts listed under Article 3 shall be submitted to the International Court of Justice, at the request of one of the Parties to the dispute.

- **The Nuremberg Statute and Crimes against Humanity**

Under the terms of the Nuremberg Statute, crimes against humanity are those aimed at a civilian population of any kind and are prohibited, whether or not they have been committed in the course of armed conflict of an international or internal nature. Crimes against humanity are described as inhuman acts of extreme gravity committed as part of a generalised or systematic attack on a civilian population of any kind, for national, political, ethnic, racial or religious reasons.

Under **Article 5 of the Statute** of the Tribunal of the Hague, crimes against humanity include assassination, extermination, enslavement, expulsion, imprisonment, torture, rape, persecution for racial, political and religious reasons and other inhuman acts *"when they are committed in the course of armed conflict of an international or internal nature".*[3]

In the territory of former Yugoslavia, crimes against humanity have also taken the form of **"ethnic cleansing"**, which consists in rendering an area ethnically homogenous through the use of force or intimidation to remove from the area in question any persons belonging to certain groups. "Ethnic cleansing" is performed using murder, torture, arbitrary arrest and imprisonment, extrajudicial execution, rape and sexual attack, enforced prostitution, forcing the civilian population into ghettos, movements, transfers and deportations of the civilian population against its will, deliberate attacks or threats against civilians in civilian areas and the indiscriminate destruction of property. These practises are clearly definable as war crimes and could also fall under the terms of the Convention on Genocide, but it will be up to the Prosecutor to define in law the act under consideration.

---

3. Unlike the Statute of Nuremberg, that of the Hague Tribunal describes as crimes against humanity those which are committed during a period of armed conflict.

Principles of international law are enshrined in the Statute of the Nuremberg Tribunal and in the judgement of that Tribunal.

In the absence of the adoption of a code covering crimes against the peace and security of humanity, general positive international law is considered to consist of the Statement of the Nuremberg Principles made in 1950 by the International Law Commission which it is worth repeating here:

Principle I

Any author of an act constituting a crime against international law is responsible on this count and liable to punishment.

Principle II

The fact that internal law does not punish an act which constitutes a crime under international law does not release the perpetrator from responsibility under international law.

Principle III

The fact that the author of an act which constitutes a crime under international law has acted in his capacity as head of State or of government does not release him from his responsibility under international law.

Principle IV

The fact of having acted on the orders of his government or those of his superior, does not release the perpetrator from responsibility under international law if he had the moral option of choice.

Principle V

Any person accused of a crime under international law has the right to a fair trial, both as regards the facts and as regards the law.

Principle VI

The crimes listed hereunder are punishable as crimes under international law.

a) Crimes against the peace:
   i.   To plan, prepare, unleash or pursue a war of aggression or a war in breach of international treaties, agreements or undertakings;
   ii. To participate in a concerted plan or plot to perpetrate any of the acts listed in paragraph i;

b) War crimes: breaches of laws and customs of war which include, but are not limited to, assassinations, ill-treatment or deportation for forced labour or any other reason of prisoner-of-war populations or persons at sea, the execution of hostages, pillage of public or private property, the perverse destruction of towns or villages or devastation which is unjustified militarily.

c) Crimes against humanity: "The assassination, extermination, enslavement, deportation or any other inhuman act committed against all the civil populations or persecutions for political, racial or religious ends, when these acts or persecutions have been committed following a crime against peace or a war crime, or in association with such crimes.

Principle VII

Complicity in a crime against peace, a war crime or a crime against humanity, as defined under principle VI, is a crime under international law.

WHO CAN BE TRIED BY THE TRIBUNAL?

Any individual
who may have committed serious breaches of human rights after 1 January, 1991 in former Yugoslavia, or who shall have prepared or encouraged such breaches, including:
• political leaders;
• commanders;
• their subordinates or those acting on their orders.

States cannot be tried
by the international criminal court for former Yugoslavia.

4. *RATIONE PERSONAE* JURISDICTION: THE GUILTY PARTIES

Under **Resolutions 808 and 827** of the Security Council, the international criminal court was set up to try those persons presumed responsible for serious breaches of international humanitarian law committed on the territory of former Yugoslavia since 1991. The expression "persons presumed responsible" designates named individuals, who alone may be considered to have criminal responsibility under international law in the present state of positive international law. Consequently, the criminal acts listed in the Statute must be performed by individuals independently of their membership of a group or citizenship of a country. Furthermore, the individuals who have perpetrated these crimes are held responsible individually. The Security Council actually ruled on this issue even before the creation of the Tribunal, for instance in resolution 771 of 13 August, 1992, when it affirmed that *"those persons who commit acts constituting serious breaches of international humanitarian law **individually** bear the responsibility"*.

Article 7 paragraph 1 of the Statute of the Tribunal states:

"whoever shall have planned, incited to commit, ordered, committed or in any other manner aided and abetted the planning, preparation or commission of a crime listed under articles 2 to 5 of the present Statute is individually responsible for the said crime".

It therefore appears that the Tribunal accepts three levels of responsibility, that of the "political leaders", that of the commanders and that of subordinates or those merely carrying out orders. The following is the distinction operated by the French Consultative Committee in its report.[4]

---

4. See Consultative Committee of French Jurists, *Report on the Creation of an International Criminal Court called upon to judge crimes committed in Former Yugoslavia.* Doc. S/25266

• Political leaders

These can be defined as the persons who originally devised the breach of the fundamental rights of the human being and the rules of war to create a system making it possible to achieve political goals. These are heads of state, heads of government and senior officials. They should be considered to be responsible for having planned, aided and abetted in planning or incited to commit crimes which fall within the Tribunal's terms of reference. The practical importance of this formula is that it includes acts which, being of a preparatory nature, would normally be excluded. Henceforward, such acts shall be considered as an automatic breach which may be suppressed independently of any trial for crimes committed by the perpetrators. Political leaders are thus responsible for having participated in the commission of the said crimes as their moral authors, instigators or organisers.

• The hierarchical command

This constitutes the intermediate level of responsibility. These are the people who give the "orders designed to perform the acts which constitute crimes". Thus, anyone giving an order to commit a crime is as guilty as the actual perpetrator of the crime. It should be emphasised that this principle has been stated already in the Geneva Conventions of 1949, which apply to both *senior officers*, whether they are at the head of regular or irregular armed forces, and to the *civilian authorities*. The responsibility of the person giving the order is thus involved irrespective of the actual commission of the crime which is the subject of the order; it is the mere fact of having chosen to "exercise his or her command in a criminal fashion" which is considered per se and which constitutes an offence in itself.

- **Their subordinates or those acting on their orders**

These have the third and lowest degree of responsibility. They are involved in their capacity as the direct perpetrators of the incriminating acts. The principle thus laid down of the existence of an individual criminal responsibility of the direct perpetrators constitutes a measure of "preventive intimidation" the aim of which is to dissuade the great possible number of subordinates from lending their support to the perpetration of such crimes. The excuse of acting under orders is thus not acceptable.

An Interview with the Deputy Prosecutor of the UN Tribunal on Former Yugoslavia

Graham Blewitt: "We shall not only be prosecuting the small fry"

THE HAGUE
By our Correspondent

The international court created by the UN to punish the violators of human rights in former Yugoslavia is on the point of being granted 11.2 million dollars for the 1994 financial year. However, if the budget for the first quarter is extrapolated to cover the whole year, this allocation would seem to be inadequate to permit the Tribunal to fulfil its mandate.

The precarious state of its finances complicates the setting up of the court, and especially choosing a site for its location, equipping the premises and hiring the necessary staff (about 100 people). The choice of the Hague as the headquarters and the status of the 11 judges have not yet been confirmed, the acting prosecutor has still not been appointed. The deputy prosecutor, the Australian, Graham Blewitt, took office on 20 February and granted us the following interview:

- *The office of the prosecutor will be the linchpin of the Tribunal. How would you organise his department?"*

The office of the prosecutor has two assignments: it has to investigate the accusations of breaches of international humanitarian law and bring the guilty to justice. There are two types of function, which are quite distinct from each other. I am currently preparing recommendations and I hope to be able to receive the first teams of investigators by mid-May, in order to launch the first phase, that of opening the inquiry.

- *How many teams do you want to set up and how would you do it?*

The budget covers about twenty investigators who could be divided into six teams, to which

should be added additional staff offered by the United Kingdom, Australia, Canada and the United States. We will need people who are accustomed to investigate serious crimes, rapes, organised crime and all forms of trafficking. That is why my preference is for experienced police officers, whether civilian or military. Then, the team of investigators needs to be of as international a nature as possible. At the moment, the best candidates come from the four countries already quoted, but I should like others, especially European ones, to come forward.

- *So, in practice, the work of the prosecutor's office has not yet begun?*

It will begin when we have enough staff — for the moment there is only me and my secretary — and when we have defined our priorities. That is the purpose of the documents we shall be receiving between now and the end of April from the Commission of experts who investigated war crimes in former Yugoslavia under the chairmanship of Mr. Bassioni, as well as Mr. Mazowiecki's reports, those of certain governments and non-governmental organisations, all of which the Tribunal will be taking over.

- *What will be your policy as far as criminal prosecutions are concerned? Where will you start to attack this mountain of atrocities?*

That is an operational matter about which I prefer to say as little as possible. However, I am convinced that certain cases of in which the Tribunal could exact punishment will show themselves to have priority. We are also beginning with blatant cases in which a lengthy investigation may not be necessary because it is important for the prosecutor to be able to move as quickly as possible

to the next phase, that of prosecutions to be brought before the courts. Finally, we know that the international community is expecting us to do more than just prosecute the "small fry".

- *Some war crimes suspects have already been arrested in Germany and Denmark. Will you be requesting their extradition?*

No. The prosecution and trial of war crimes in former Yugoslavia is a huge task which the Tribunal does not claim to be able to perform alone. It is important for the countries of Europe who may be harbouring these criminals among the refugees and for them to bring them to trial themselves and the German and Danish trials which we are monitoring closely, may be an encouragement. Do not forget that the reason why the UN created this Tribunal is because history is littered with examples of countries which did nothing about such crimes. If the Tribunal had existed prior to the ethnic cleansing operations, perhaps the political leaders would have thought twice about performing them.

- *But the creation of the Tribunal has not stopped the pursuance of the war and its excesses?*

That is true. It is thinkable, and regrettable, that the slowness with which the Tribunal has been set up may have encouraged the belligerents to continue with the same course of action.

- *Aren't you afraid that the abolition, or indefinite postponement of the court might be made a condition for a comprehensive peace process?*

Better to have no peace at all than peace at that price.

Interviewer: Christian CHARTIER
Le Monde, 9 April, 1994.

III. PROCEDURE

In order to make the various stages of the proceedings more visible, we are presenting them in diagrammatic form. This procedural diagram does not include the situation in which the accused is absent. This will be covered in the third part of the document.

(See the diagram at the end of this publication).

• **Additional specifications**

JOINDER AND DISJOINDER OF CASES

If persons are accused of the same offence or different offences committed on the **same occasion, Article 48 of the Rules** deals with the possibility of indicting them and trying them together, each accused having the same rights as if he or she had been tried separately. This constitutes a joinder of cases.

However, *"in order to prevent any conflict of interests which might cause serious damage to an accused or to safeguard the interest of justice"*, Article 50 states that *"the lower court may order a separate trial for each of any accused whose cases have been joined"*.

Joinder of indictments

If the incriminating acts were committed **on the same occasion** and by the **same accused, Article 50 of the Rules** considers that they may be the subject of a single bill of indictment.

Both the joinder of cases and the joinder of indictments make it possible to manage the proceedings more efficiently, to the extent that several cases can be tries simultaneously, while still respecting the rights of the defence. They also make it possible to highlight the seriousness of the violation of international humanitarian law. Furthermore, the joinder of indictments or counts make it possible to emphasise the overall responsibility of a single person for several crimes. It is also a means of protecting the victim because he or she will no longer have to face his or her attacker alone, so the individual role of the plaintiff is reduced.

Putting War Criminals on Trial

by Boutros Boutros-Ghali*

The International Court which has been assigned the task of judging the perpetrators of the breaches of humanitarian law committed in former Yugoslavia is being set up this Wednesday, 17 November, in the Hague. For the first time, since the Nuremberg Tribunal, war criminals will be punished under international law. It is quite unacceptable, in fact, that the sort of acts which we are unfortunate enough to witness so frequently and which revolt our consciences should have remained unpunished for so long.

I should like to emphasise, in the most solemn way possible, the importance which I attribute to this Tribunal. I insist on saying so all the more because the construction of an international society governed by the rule of law is a slow, modest and chaotic creation. It cannot satisfy either the sensation-seekers or those who want instant gratification. And yet, it is this patient progress towards international standards which most surely indicate the stages of evolution of universal morality.

The creation of the Tribunal is exemplary in every aspect. The Security Council, at my behest, decided to create this Tribunal itself. On the basis of Chapter VII of the UN Charter, that is to say in order to create an international condemnation. This is a precedent the importance of which deserves to be highlighted. By deciding to use a resolution as the basis for its foundation, the Security Council has insisted on showing its desire to act quickly. War crimes ought to be subject to the rule of law as quickly as possible. While a bitter war continues to be fought in former Yugoslavia, the law is already at work to condemn those who have violated its most elementary rules.

Furthermore, in acting thus, the Security Council wanted to show as clearly as possible that henceforward, war crimes and the systematic breach of human rights constitute genuine threats to peace and must be treated as such.

The Security Council also wanted to confirm that it was acting in the name of the international community as a whole. All the member States of the United Nations are required to co-operate in the application of international sanctions. They thus must do their utmost to ensure that the court is able to fulfil its mission.

The desire to make the court truly international is expressed in its very composition. The General Assembly of the United Nations has been charged with electing the prosecutor and judges. Through its vote, it has given the widest possible and most universal basis to the new institution. The prosecutor, Ramón Escovar-Salom is Venezuelan and the 11 judges are American, Australian, Canadian, Chinese, Costa Rican, Egyptian, French, Italian, Malaysian, Nigerian and Pakistani. Thus, it is a truly international community which has set itself up as a whole to judge the war crimes committed in former Yugoslavia.

These crimes have long been condemned under international law. The Geneva Conventions for the protection of war victims, the Convention for the prevention and suppression of the Crime of Genocide, the Hague Convention of 1907 on the laws and customs of War as well as the principles of Nuremberg all contributed to the creation of a truly international set of humanitarian laws. In its day, Yugoslavia also ratified these texts. So this is not a case, as at Nuremberg, of applying the law retroactively to conquered enemies. In this case, it is a matter of the application of standards which are known and recognised by the principle parties involved. No institution existed to do this. The Tribunal concerning former Yugoslavia is an example for the future.

Human Rights Diplomacy

In fact, its mandate opens up radically new perspectives on the method of repression used against war crimes. All those who have actually committed such crimes are liable to prosecution by the jurisdiction of the Tribunal. The Tribunal is also empowered to try all those who participated, whether close at hand or from afar, in the planning and preparation of the breaches of human rights.

The world in which the UN has to take action is radically different from that which emerged in the aftermath of the Second World War and which was imposed during the Cold War. It is not merely a case today of maintaining peace between state by respecting their individual sovereignty. The conflicts which divide and split people within the same states must be confronted. It is these new conflicts which are currently the greatest threat to international peace and which attack human rights most violently. They force us to invent new responses and to find new solutions. The creation of a diplomacy of democracy And human rights is one of the major challenges of our time. In this action, the creation of the international Tribunal takes all it place and all its value.

*Secretary General of the United Nations Organisation

Thursday, 18 November, 1993
POINT OF VIEW

II.
AID, PROTECTION AND FACILITIES AVAILABLE TO VICTIMS AND WITNESSES

I FINANCIAL AND INSTITUTIONAL ASPECTS OF AID AND PROTECTION

1. THE NEED FOR AN ADEQUATE BUDGET

At the time of writing, the Tribunal has a budget of about 200,000 ECU for the protection of victims and witnesses, to cover a six-month period. This initial sum is the result of a provisional arrangement with the **European Community.** In fact, a draft agreement with that organisation is currently being negotiated for overall funding for a longer period. This application for funding has to be made to the European Community through an intermediary, the Centre for the Rehabilitation of Victims of Torture, situated in Copenhagen, which is responsible for passing on monies allocated to the Tribunal.

2. THE DISTRIBUTION OF AID TO VICTIMS AND WITNESSES

Article 34 of the Rules of the Tribunal states:

"(A) *The Registrar[5] shall create a Victim and Witness Aid Division consisting of qualified personnel who shall be responsible for (i) recommending the adoption of protective measures for victims and witnesses in accordance with Article 22 of the Statute; (ii) supplying advice and assistance to the victims and witnesses, especially in cases of rape and sexual attack.*

(B) *When staff for this Division are recruited, the need to employ women who have had specialist training shall be duly taken into account"*.

At the time of writing, this Division has not yet been set up, only a working party has been created to consider the ways in which it will operate and produce proposals to this effect. We shall thus limit ourselves to making a few suggestions as to what this department could or should be.

Clearly this Division must provide **psychological aid** to victims and witnesses whenever they intervene (before the prosecutor has started questioning them or once the case has been opened).

Prior to the court case, it ought to play the role of a **support service** (offering information about victims' and witnesses' rights, protective measures from which they could benefit, etc.) as well as **advice** for compiling a case with a view to informing the Prosecutor accordingly and choosing the competent jurisdiction (the national courts or the international court). This role is all the more necessary since an associated network cannot cover it adequately. In this last point, it is important to recruit the NGOs

---

5. It was originally foreseen that this Division would be attached to the Prosecutor's office, but it was attached to the Registrar for reasons of neutrality and the administration of fair justice.

to this task, that is to say after a thorough evaluation of the responsibilities they undertake to assume, and they must promise long-term commitment to the project.

Once the case has been opened in the international criminal court, the Division must inform the victim of the progress of the proceedings in which he or she is involved (since victims cannot be represented by counsel at court and for this reason are completely kept at a distance from the case in progress). The Division must also cover the logistical aspect of the protection of victims and witnesses. It would be appropriate for a place to be created in which their physical protection would be assured. In this respect, discussions with representatives of the Dutch government are in progress for a forthcoming agreement concerning the creation of a **"safe house"**.

II PROTECTION GIVEN TO VICTIMS AND WITNESSES: INDISPENSABLE BUT STILL INADEQUATE

The protection of victims and witnesses must constitute one of the fundamental preoccupations of the international Tribunal because it is only their participation, in the widest sense of the term, which will give the necessary impetus to the commitment to pursue criminal prosecutions against the authors of the serious breaches of international humanitarian law and trying those responsible.

If the Tribunal is to ensure genuine protection for the victims and witnesses **throughout the whole length of the trial**, including during the preliminary investigation, its members have to consider the need to take protective measures for the **phases preceding and subsequent to the trial**. Unlike the second phase (preparation and trial) during which protection is the direct responsibility of the court, in the two other phases this has to become the objective of close collaboration with NGOs.

It is necessary, however, to put the nature of such protection in a suitable context. The court, like any other institution, cannot guarantee victims and witnesses complete and unfailing protection. It cannot foresee all the risks which might be involved, especially within the context of the armed conflict still raging on the territory of former Yugoslavia. **In this context, any decision to inform the Tribunal or to testify before it involves and inevitable component of risk.** Furthermore, the Tribunal cannot ensure effective protection for members of a victim's or witness's family who have stayed behind in former Yugoslavia. Members of the Tribunal are also aware of the crucial problem of the return of victims and witnesses to their own communities. It must be emphasised here that defence witnesses are not excluded from the system of protection which has been established. The limited financial resources allocated to the Tribunal for victim protection explains this distinction.

Due to the special circumstances linked to the conflict in former Yugoslavia, **the necessary protection of victims and witnesses and the equally necessary respect for the rights of the defence, would appear to be two imperatives which are difficult to reconcile** but which the Tribunal must tackle. The adoption and implementation of protective measures must respond to the initiation of a balance between these two requirements. The legitimacy and credibility of the criminal court depends on them.

It is also necessary to emphasize that it is the evidence which the victim can provide and not the damage he or she has suffered which are important in the eyes of the court. In this respect, the tribunal is not different from any other criminal court. The action brought before such courts has the primary objective of condemning a breach of national or international public order, one which constitutes a crime. This action has a penal nature which justifies the fact that a victim can only be considered in his or her capacity as a witness and not as a person who has the right to compensation for the harm suffered. This is distinct from the purely civil action the purpose of which is to re-establish, through financial compensation or reparations in kind, the *status quo ante*.

Thus, the concept of the victim as someone entitled to reparations for the damage inflicted upon him or her disappears, **purely in the context of criminal proceedings**, in favour of the concept of **witness-victim** capable of producing proof of the existence of a crime. However, contrary to the ordinary criminal jurisdictions which permit civil action to be taken alongside criminal proceedings, **this court forbids the bringing of a civil action.** Neither the victims, nor any NGO acting on behalf of a victim, may institute civil proceedings before the Tribunal. The Tribunal refers such actions back to the national jurisdictions.[6]

1. EXPLICIT AND DIRECT PROTECTION: THE INADEQUACIES

The expression "explicit and direct protection" covers protective measures which are mentioned expressly in the Rules of the Tribunal, of which victims and witnesses are the direct beneficiaries. These measures respond to two separate but complementary objectives, namely to protect the physical and moral integrity of the individual and facilitate the giving of his or her evidence.

- **First objective: protecting the physical and moral integrity of victims and witnesses**

The first of these objectives is taken into account in articles 40, 60, 75 and 79 of the Rules.

According to **Article 40**, "in emergency situations, the Prosecutor may ask any state (...) to take any measure necessary in order to prevent (...) the intimidation or attack on the physical integrity of victims or witnesses (...)". **Article 69** states, "*in exceptional cases, the Prosecutor may ask the lower court to order that the identity of a victim or a witness not be divulged in order to prevent their being in danger or running risks and this*

---

6. As regards compensation for victims, see Part III (I,b).

shall be done until they are placed under the protection of the Tribunal (...)".

Article 75 also makes it possible to take *"appropriate measures for the protection of the private life and the security of victims or witnesses (...)".* This refers mainly to measures *"of such a nature as to prevent the revelation to the public or the press of the identity of a victim or witness, any person related to or associated with them or the place in which they are to be found, using such means as removing the name of the person concerned from the court records and removing indications which would make it possible to identify such a person, prevention of public access to any exhibit in the case which might make it possible to identify the victim (...), the use of an alias".* Article 75 also considers that in case of need the lower court should also *"monitor the questioning procedures in order to prevent any form of harassment or intimidation".* This last provision applies equally to the victim or witness and to the accused.

Finally, under **Article 79**, *"in order to ensure protection of a victim or witness or to prevent the revelation of his or her identity"*, the lower court may order that sessions of the court be held **in camera.**

If the identity of the victim or witness can never be divulged to the public, it must be made known to the accused and his or her legal representative as soon as the victim or witness is placed under the protection of the court in order to respect the rights of the defence.

- **Second objective: to facilitate the evidence of victims and witnesses**

The second objective, which is to facilitate the evidence "*of a vulnerable victim or witness*", is dealt with in **Articles 71(D) and 75 of the Rules**, which cover the use of certain technical resources, such as "*videoconferencing, alteration of image or voice, the use of unidirectional close circuit television*".

These various measures would appear to be satisfactory in their content both on the level of the protection they consider affording as on that of respecting the rights of the defence (on the latter point, Article 75-(A) specifies that "*the said measures do not affect the rights of the accused*"). However, they must be completed in order to attain an optimal degree of protection. In fact, under article 69-(A), for example, the protection of the identity of a victim or witness is lifted at the moment in which they are placed under the protection of the Tribunal. On could question the meaning of the phrase "protection of the Tribunal" and the procedures used to implement it.

2. EXPLICIT BUT INDIRECT PROTECTION

The terms "explicit and indirect protection" are used to designate measures expressly covered by the Rules as they apply to the accused. This set of measures covers the conditions under which the accused is remanded in custody,[7] conditions which may be altered on the basis of the requirements linked to the protection of victims and witnesses.

---

7. A prison has been placed at the disposal of the tribunal by the Dutch authorities. For more information about the conditions of detention, see the Rule governing the prison regime for persons awaiting trial or appeal before the Tribunal or remanded on the order of the Tribunal, IT/38/Rev.3, 10 May, 1994.

The Rule adopts the principle of **preventive detention** of any person named in a bill of indictment and having been transferred to the headquarters of the international court. *"The accused is remanded in a location made available by the host country (...)"* (see **Article 64**). This principle is reinforced by the conditions of bail because under Article 65 of the Rules, bail is only to be granted *"under exceptional circumstances and to the extent that (the lower court) is certain that the accused will attend court and, if released, **shall not endanger a victim, witness or any other person**. The lower court may impose any conditions of bail that it considers appropriate, including the payment of a bond and where appropriate, the fulfilment of the conditions necessary in order to guarantee the presence of the accused at the trial **and the protection of other parties**"*. This provision is proof that the Tribunal considers itself to be under an obligation to protect victims and witnesses.

Similarly, **Article 99**, concerning the status of a person who has been acquitted, also contains provisions covering such protection, since it states, *"In case of an acquittal, the accused is released. However, **should an appeal be lodged** during the hearing by the Prosecutor **as soon as such acquittal has been pronounced**, the court may issue an **arrest warrant**, at the Prosecutor's behest, naming the accused which shall take **immediate effect** (...)"*.

This provision in no way affects the rights of the defence, but is the logical consequence of the suspensive effect of means of appeal. This means that in the case of an appeal lodged against a judgement by the lower court, the implementation of such judgement is suspended until the appeal judgement has been handed down. The indeterminate nature of this judgement then makes it possible to place a person in preventive detention even if they have been acquitted. It should also be emphasised that preventive detention of a person who has been acquitted is an option which the Tribunal may use but not an obligation.

3. THE QUESTION OF PROTECTION OF VICTIMS AND WITNESSES FROM NATIONAL JURISDICTIONS[8]

The question of victim and witness protection before national jurisdictions depends on the law of each state. In this respect, those rules of internal criminal law which offer such protection therefore deserve to be examined. For example, in French criminal law there are provisions which offer indirect protection to victims and witnesses.

Under France's **New Code of Criminal Procedure** (N.C.P.), the act of committing a murder (**Art. 221-4**), to submit a person to torture or acts of barbarism (**Art. 222-3**), to cause death unintentionally by means of an assault (**Art. 222-8**) and to commit an assault resulting in permanent (**Art 222-10**) or temporary (**Art. 222-12** and **222-13**) incapacity *"on a witness, victim or civil party, either to prevent him or her from denouncing actions, from lodging a complaint or from giving evidence, or as a result of such denunciation, complaint or deposition"*, constitutes *"grounds for aggravation of the penalty involved"*.

Furthermore, according to **Article 434-15 of the N.C.P.**, *"the fact of using promises, offers, presents, pressure, threats, actions, manoeuvres or ruses during proceedings or with a view to an application to the courts or by the defence in order to force another person to either make or produce a mendacious deposition, statement or evidence (...)"* constitutes an offence in itself: suborning of witnesses.

Furthermore, **Article 144** of the **Code of Criminal Procedure** states:. *"(...) remand in custody can be ordered or "extended" where the remand in custody of the "person under interrogation" is the sole way of preserving proof or material*

---

8. Since the Statute and the Rules of the Tribunal do not exclude the fact that a trial can be held under national jurisdictions, the question of victim and witness protection must also be covered herein.

indicators or where it serves to prevent pressure being exerted on witnesses of victims (...)".

III. LIGHTENING THE BURDEN OF PROOF: THE EXAMPLE OF SEXUAL ASSAULT

Sexual assault constitutes an important area of the crimes committed on the territory of former Yugoslavia. It emerges from reading the various reports produced by international bodies that *"rape was used during the conflict in former Yugoslavia as a weapon of war"*.[9]

In this respect, Tadeusz Mazowiecki[10] in his various reports as rapporteur of the United Nations Commission on Human Rights, denounced "rape as an instrument of ethnic cleansing".

Amnesty International, for its part, has written that *"rape and sexual torture, generally inflicted on Moslem women by the Serbian forces, took place in a number of places in Bosnia-Herzegovina and in some cases, these acts were committed in an organised and systematic way, with the women being deliberately*

---

9. *Le Livre noir de l'ex-Yougoslavie*, Ethnic Cleansing and War Crimes, Documents collected by the Nouvel Observateur and Reporters Sans Frontière. Paris, Le Seuil, Arléa, 1993, 485 pp.

10. Mr. Mazowiecki, the special rapporteur for the Commission on Human Rights, went out into the field on several occasions. He compiled 12 reports which all indicate that atrocities have been committed in former Yugoslavia.

EXTRACT FROM THE FIFTH REPORT OF MR. TADEUSZ MAZOWIECKI TO THE U.N. COMMISSION OF HUMAN RIGHTS[11]

Rape is an act whereby the rapist, using force and compulsion, seeks to humiliate, dishonour, vilify and terrify the victim. In all his reports, the special Rapporteur highlighted the diversity of the methods used to achieve ethnic cleansing. Rape is one of these methods, as was said at the beginning. In this context, rape is not only a crime committed against the person of the victim, it also aims to humiliate, dishonour, vilify and terrify the whole group. Reliable information has reported instances of public rape, for example in front of a whole village, to terrorise the population and force ethnic groups to flee.

In the opinion of the special Rapporteur, it is not currently possible to determine the number of rape victims within the context of this conflict. However, it is clear that the victims are numerous and that the first priority must be to help them.

---

11. Cf. Doc E/CN.4/1993/50 p.19

WHAT IS THE U.N. COMMISSION ON HUMAN RIGHTS?

The Commission on Human Rights is a subsidiary body attached to the Economic and Social Council (ECOSOC). It was created in 1946 on the basis of Article 68 of the United Nations Charter. It consists of 53 member States in the United Nations, meets six times a year in Geneva in February and March. The representatives of the member States who sit on the commission are appointed by their governments and act upon their instructions. The Commission on Human Rights is thus, by its very nature, a political organisation.

Initially, the Commission's mandate only gave it the right to formulate proposals to ECOSOC concerning the creation of international human rights instruments. Subsequently, thanks to ECOSOC resolution 1235 (XLII) of 6 June, 1967, it was authorised *"to examine information concerning flagrant human rights breaches and breaches of basic freedoms"*. This resolution gives the Commission the opportunity to initiate extensive investigations of situations of constant and systematic human rights breaches. It is on this basis that the Commission instituted public proceedings, called special proceedings, which focus on particular countries or, since 1980, on particular issues. Today, 12 special proceedings on issues and 13 special proceedings on countries are currently being conducted.

At the same time, the Commission created a confidential procedure, by adopting Resolution 1503 (XLVIII) on 27 May, 1970, making it possible to perform a confidential investigation of *"any communication which appears to reveal a set of flagrant and systematic breaches"*. These communications emanate from individuals or non-governmental organisations.

held captive with a view of rape and sexual torture. These incidents appear to form part of a much greater plan for waging the war, including the intimidation and exactions of Moslems and Croatians, thus causing thousands of them to flee or to obey the orders expelling them from their home territory, for fear of more violence. The question of knowing whether rape was deliberately chosen by the political and military leaders as a weapon against their adversaries remains a moot point. *What is certain is that hitherto, effective measures have rarely been taken (if at all) against such exactions and those responsible at a local level, both politically and militarily, must have known and in general approved of the rape and sexual violence against women (...). These exactions, including sexual violence against women, were committed by all parties to the conflict. Amnesty International is aware that the Croatian armed forces in Bosnia-Herzegovina also raped and committed sexual crimes against women, although on a much smaller scale".*[12]

The nature of these crimes produce, **an almost insurmountable trauma,** in the victim, especially when it is amplified by the massive and systematic way in which it is practised. In this respect, Jadranka Cacic-Kumpes, a Croatian academic, explains that *"These women and girls have to confront daily, alone and in deep shock, the problems of being refugees as well as their internal dilemmas, aggravated by feelings of degradation, shame and a whole series of prejudices created by their patriarchal upbringing (...). The resulting stigma of rape is thus felt by the victims at several complex levels (...). Such terrible events not only affect the re-integration of raped women into*

---

12. Amnesty International report: "Rape and sexual violence practised by the armed forces in Bosnia-Herzegovina" dated 21 January, 1993 in The Black Book of Former Yugoslavia, Ethnic Cleansing and War Crimes, op. cit.

society but also the children which might be born from such circumstances".[13]

The scale of these cruelties was taken into account by the United Nations when it formulated the Statute and Rules of the Tribunal. The specific nature of these crimes is the reason for special rules governing evidence in matters of sexual violence.

Throughout a criminal trial, it is the job of the person lodging the complaint to provide proof of the existence of an act constituting an offence, the defendant being presumed innocent until guilt is established, that is to say when the verdict is pronounced. The international Tribunal is not exception to this rule but it is considering lightening the burden of proof. It also restricts the range of defences open to the accused.

Article 96 of the Rules of the Tribunal states:

"In cases of sexual violence:

(i) *Witness corroboration of the evidence of the victim's evidence is not required;*

(ii) *Consent cannot be used as a defence, where the victim: (a) has been subjected to acts of violence of if she was forced, imprisoned or subjected to psychological pressure or if she feared being subjected to the same or if she was threatened with such acts, or (b) if she considered it reasonable that if she did not submit another woman might be subjected to such acts, or be threatened or forced out of fear;*

(iii) *the prior sexual behaviour of the victim cannot be invoked as a defence".*

---

13. Document presented during the East-West Conference, "Women in a Europe in Transition, the Rights of Immigrant and Refugee Women", Athens, November, 1992.

Article 96(i) is an indisputable lightening of the burden of proof for the victim. In fact, it appears that even if the witness's evidence is rather weak in establishing the facts, neither the court nor the defence can force her to corroborate the truth of the evidence through that of a third party. If, in view of the evidence already gathered, it appears that sexual crimes were committed, in most cases, in the presence of other people, this provision could constitute an attack on the rights of the defence in cases where only the victim and the accused were present at the time of the incriminating events. Proof of the commission of the crime would then rest solely on comparing the victim's allegations with the case being put by the accused. This problem could attain a scope which it would be difficult to control in the context of ethnic cleansing occurring at the end of the war. One might ask oneself to what extent Article 96(i) could represent an opportunity for each of the parties to the conflict to use the Tribunal as an instrument of political cleansing with regard to certain of their own people. The only guarantee for the accused rests on the Prosecutor's supreme evaluation as to the opportunity for prosecution and that of the judges as to their legal interpretation of the facts.

Article 96(ii) for its part constitutes a restriction of the defences which can be employed by the accused. In its first draft, Article 96(ii), states *"The victim's consent cannot be invoked as a defence"*, which means that whatever the nature of the consent even if this were given freely and voluntarily, it can under no circumstance be used as a defence. This provision would constitute such an attack on the rights of the accused that the judges amended it so that the concept of consent was modified where it cannot be used as a defence. Henceforward, only consent extracted under physical or moral constraint cannot be invoked. This new version respects the rights of the accused.

Article 96(iii) also constitutes a restriction of the means of defence, but unlike the previous provision, it poses a problem with regard to respect for the rights of the accused. In fact it is debatable whether an accused may freely invoke the arguments which he might wish to put forward as his defence. One could also question the relevance and usefulness of such an article, to the extent where the judges are in any case the sole authority in judging the facts.

58

World Affairs
INTERVIEW WITH PIERRE TRUCHE

The Weapon of International Law against War Crimes

Is this the advent of "humanitarian justice"? With the establishment of an international Tribunal to judge war crimes committed in former Yugoslavia, as regards international law ...and coercion.

Voted in unanimously with the noted support of the Russians, Resolution 808 deals with the trials of those presumed to be responsible for *"serious breaches of international humanitarian law"*. The technical arrangements and the operational methods of the Court, which will have jurisdiction over the whole of former Yugoslavia have not yet been clearly defined but the Secretary-General of the United Nations is to announce them within two months time on the basis of the recommendations of a group of experts in international law.

Forty-seven years after Nuremberg, the creation of such a tribunal has nevertheless caused certain political and legalistic reservations to be expressed. Pierre Truche, the chief prosecutor of the court of appeal and chairman of the committee established to create the international tribunal, answers questions put by Le Point.

Pierre Truche: Even if this Tribunal only tries cases involving former Yugoslavia, it indubitably represents a major advance in international law. This discussion has preoccupied jurists throughout the 20th century. After the 1914-1918 War, several attempts were made to create an international tribunal. Then there was the Nuremberg Tribunal and the Tokyo Tribunal. Today we have finally reached a new stage.

Le Point: What are the legal foundations for convictions for war crimes?

At Nuremberg, a convention was signed by the Soviets, the

Former Yugoslavia:
For the first time, the creation of a special tribunal may facilitate the re-establishment of peace in the war zone

Americans, the French and the British. Today, the UN has chosen another method, based on Chapter VII of the Charter which authorises recourse to force. Especially as international law has made considerable progress, especially with the right of interference. For the first time, it has been realised that the creation of a special tribunal could facilitate the re-establishment of peace in a war zone.

However, the resolution only mentions "serious breaches of international humanitarian law"...

Humanitarian law has a very special resonance. Each war creates progress in humanitarian law. Since 1945, several Conventions have been signed including those of 1949. The later give a detailed list of the serious breaches to be condemned.

Are we witnessing recognition that there is such a thing as "humanitarian justice"?

At least this is a form of justice which condemns breaches of international law. The Geneva Conventions were accepted by almost every country, including Yugoslavia. What was not planned was an international tribunal.

Is it possible to sentence war criminals before victors and vanquished have emerged from the conflict?

Should only the vanquished be prosecuted? Serious breaches are also committed by victors. What counts is to determine the breach and identify the perpetrators. We

are now looking backwards, even before the end of the conflict, contrary to Nuremberg. And one day you will have to go further and create a tribunal with a preventive role prior to any conflict.

How would such a tribunal operate?

The terrain has already been mapped out. France, in particular, has already recommended the presence of specialists in criminal international law and experts from human rights organisation, such as the International Court of Justice, the European Court of Human Rights, etc., especially concerning the rights of the defence. But the question that causes the most difficulties is that of whether trials can be conducted in absentia.

Isn't there a contradiction in the effort to bring the political leaders to trial and the bringing of such leaders to sit down at the negotiating table?

The committee of jurists distinguished three levels of responsibility, namely, those who devised criminal policies, the intermediaries and those who carried them out. So the political leaders cannot be left on one side. The work of the jurists consists of locating the accused and bringing them to trial. There is no automatic responsibility however, each case must be judged on its own merits. This tribunal ought to have a preventive and deterrent role.

Shall we ever see the creation of a permanent tribunal for the judgement of war crimes?

We are progressing from the theory of law to its practice. The most important thing is the political will,which exists. It must be used so that war crimes do not remain unpunished.

(Interview by Olivier Weber)

27 February 1993 LE POINT Number 1067

III.
THE CRUX OF THE MATTER: TRYING THE CRIMINALS

I. TRYING THE CRIMINALS: COOPERATION FROM STATES IS A NECESSITY

The Tribunal for judging the criminals in former Yugoslavia can only operate effectively if countries have the **political will** to cooperate with it. These countries must regard the Tribunal as an instrument in the service of their global jurisdiction and not as an attack on their national sovereignty.

If international law considers that the state best placed to enforce the law is that which has territorial, individual or real jurisdiction, in the special context of the situation in former Yugoslavia, these rules of attribution of jurisdiction cannot basically be applied.

Furthermore, the inability or lack of desire of the countries of former Yugoslavia and the inertia of other countries as regards the punishment of serious breaches of humanitarian international law make it vital to create an international legal instrument capable of federating these jurisdictions.

1. THE APPORTIONMENT OF JURISDICTIONS BETWEEN THE TRIBUNAL AND THE NATIONAL JURISDICTIONS

a. The existence of competing jurisdictions

National jurisdictions may exercise their competence in criminal matters on the basis of several principles contained in national law and/or recognised under international law.

Under the principle of the **territoriality** of criminal law, the State on whose territory the crime was committed has jurisdiction over it. This principle is generally applied by States and this tendency to try crimes in the area in which they were committed was confirmed by the Nuremberg Statute concerning crimes committed in a particular geographical area.

In addition to the principle of territoriality, there are other principles, and especially that of the **personality** of the criminal law. This principle can be interpreted in two different ways depending on whether one is considering the perpetrator or the victim.

If one takes the perpetrator of the breach into consideration, one is dealing with an **active personality**. This would mean that the court of the country of which the perpetrator is a national would have jurisdiction even if the crime had been committed on the territory of a different state. The principle of **passive personality**, on the other hand, recognises the competence of the court of the nationality of the victim of the breach.

In the Lotus case, the permanent International Court of Justice implicitly referred to the system of the personality of criminal law. It stated that *"it is true that the principle of territoriality in criminal law is the basis for all legislation and it is no less true that all or almost all such legislations extend their application to offences committed outside their territory, even where the criminal justice system itself varies from state to state. The territoriality of criminal law is thus not an absolute principle in international law, and can in no way be confused with territorial sovereignty*". [14]

Finally, quite apart from territorial jurisdiction and the system of personality of the criminal law, the criminal courts of a state may have jurisdiction even if there is nothing to attach the crime committed to the country in question. Thus, **universal jurisdiction** is typical of a system which authorises the criminal courts of any country to try the perpetrator of a serious breach of international humanitarian law due to the seriousness nature of the crime, regardless of the place in which the crime was committed, its nature and its perpetrator. [15]

States must practise universal competence because it alone makes it possible to prosecute crimes in the absence of extradition. That is the logical consequence of the law of *aut dedere, aut judicare*, which obliges a state on whose territory the criminal happens to be to extradite him or her if it considers itself unable to try him or her or does not wish to do so.

It would thus appear that States (the States of former Yugoslavia, in application of territorial jurisdiction or the system of personality; all the other States by virtue of the principle of universal jurisdiction) are undeniably competent to try those responsible for serious breaches of international humanitarian law committed on the territory of former Yugoslavia. Such exclusive exercise of their jurisdiction has nevertheless encountered objections.

All the crimes to be punished were committed within the geographical boundaries of former Yugoslavia, so the application of the principle of territoriality would seem to grant jurisdiction to the courts of former Yugoslavia – the Bosnian, Croatian or

---

14. See C.P.J.I., Collection of judgements, Series A-N• 10, Judgement N• 9, 7 September, 1927, p. 20

15. Guillaume, G., *Terrorisme et droit international*, R.C.A.D.I. III, 215 p. 348

Serbian jurisdictions, to be precise. However, the condition of the
institutions in some of the countries concerned and the war
currently raging on their territories makes the possibility of
effective prosecutions highly unlikely. The same applies to any
application of the system of personality. Furthermore, by
recognising the jurisdiction of the state of which the perpetrator is
a national (active personality) would amount, in certain cases, to
granting that state the right to judge its own political leaders who
might have ordered or organised or tolerated the criminal activity.
On the other hand, recognition of the jurisdiction of the state
whose nationals were the victims (passive personality) would not
appear to offer sufficient guarantees of impartiality and
objectivity. As for the application of the universal jurisdiction, if
it has the advantage of participating in the introduction of an
international criminal code which is less bound by the law and
order of a particular nation and less subjected to its rules, applied
as such it would not be able to deal with the need for an effective
exercise of the repressive measures against those convicted of
serious breaches of international humanitarian law.

However, despite these objections, the Security Council has
not excluded the possibility of cooperation from national
jurisdictions. The question then arises of how the problem of the
simultaneous exercise of national and international jurisdictions
can be solved.

b. The principle of primacy and the ways in which it is applied

- **The combination of the *non bis in idem* (double jeopardy) principle with that of primacy and the relinquishing of jurisdiction**

This is a principle which makes it possible to resolve positive
conflicts of jurisdiction (positive conflicts of jurisdiction are those
in which two or more jurisdictions belonging to different

HOW IS THE PRINCIPLE OF
NON BIS IN IDEM APPLIED WHERE
THERE IS AN INTERNATIONAL JURISDICTION
AND NATIONAL JURISDICTIONS?

- **If the international criminal court has already tried an accused**

  * *if a national court intends to retry the accused*:
    - the international criminal court shall ask the national court to abandon the prosecution
  * *if the national court ignores this demand to stop the prosecution*:
    - the Security Council is duly informed.

- **If a national court has already tried an accused**

  * *in principle:*
    - the international criminal court can no longer deal with the matter
  * *the exceptions:*
    - unless the crime is defined as a crime under common law
    - unless the national court has not respected the principles of independence and impartiality
    - unless the national trial was intended to extricate accused from his/her international criminal responsibility
    - unless the prosecution was not pursued with diligence.

sovereign States are competent to consider the same acts by virtue of the international rules of attribution of jurisdiction applicable thereto, such as, for example, the principle of territoriality and that of personality). This principle exists both in criminal law and in international law and is intended to ensure that no one is tried twice for the same offence. In international law, the application of the principle of *non bis in idem*, a principle enshrined in **Article 14 §7 of the 1966 International Covenant on Civil and Political Rights** which constitutes a guarantee in procedural matters for an individual arrested or held in custody for a criminal offence, by protecting him or her from *"the unfair consequences resulting from the accretion of repressive national jurisdictions if they are liable to lead to an accretion of convictions and punishments"*.[16]

If the *non bis idem* principle makes it possible to resolve problems of conflicting jurisdictions between national jurisdictions, it is not applicable in the present case because the Tribunal is not a foreign jurisdiction but an international one. Consequently, the principle is inapplicable from the outset. It must be combined with that of the recognised priority of an international judgement in application of the **principle of primacy of international law over national law.** But for reasons of effectiveness and so as to avoid totally depriving States of their jurisdiction in terms of criminal law, it would be a good idea not to rule out a national jurisdiction completely if it were to prove more effective than an international one.

These various requirements were taken into account when the Statute of the International Tribunal was compiled.

Thus, **Article 9 of the Statute** lays down the principle of the primacy of an international tribunal over national jurisdictions, the former being capable at any stage of the proceedings to ask the latter to defer to it. It should be noted in passing that nothing has

---

16. Letter to the Chairman of the Security Council from the Permanent French Representative to the United Nations. Doc. S/25266.

been planned as regards the possibility of the Tribunal deferring to a national penal regime.

Article 10 of the Statute applies the principle of *non bis in idem* as follows: if a person has already been tried by the international tribunal (for actions constituting serious breaches of international humanitarian law), he or she cannot be committed to a national jurisdiction even for the same offences. Conversely, a judgement pronounced by a national jurisdiction for the above-mentioned offence(s) excludes any later proceedings before an international criminal court, on condition that certain circumstances to be dealt with below, do not apply.

- **Problems posed by the practise of referral back**

Article 9 of the Rules covers the referral back from a national jurisdiction to the Tribunal if "(i) *the offence has been treated as a felony under common law; (ii) if the proceedings adopted are unlikely to be either impartial nor independent and are designed to relieve the accused of his or her international criminal responsibility or shall not have been pursued with diligence,* or (iii) *the subject of the proceedings covers actions or points of law which affect investigations or prosecutions currently before the Tribunal.*"

It should be noted that a case is only referred back where the proceedings undertaken before a national jurisdiction is in operation.

A few observations are appropriate here concerning the referral back procedure as covered by the Rules.

It must first be emphasised that the practise of referral back, which is governed by strict conditions, is unlikely to involve the jurisdictions of the countries of former Yugoslavia. Unfortunately, it is likely that, under the circumstances, the criminal courts of those countries will be unable to offer sufficient guarantees of impartiality and objectivity. It should not be forgotten that one of the arguments in favour of the creation of an *ad hoc* international tribunal was to compensate for the lack of reaction by the countries in question to the crimes perpetrated on their territory. As for other countries, the problems considered above are unlikely to arise, since the procedure for referring a case back to a national jurisdiction will only be used in rare cases.

However, Article 9 (iii) of the Rule permits the Prosecutor to investigate the case even if the conditions covered by articles 9 (i) and 9(ii) will not prevail and the national jurisdiction in question objects to the matter being removed from it.

Furthermore, a problem might arise as to whether an international tribunal is kept informed of proceedings in progress before national jurisdictions, since there is no requirement for States to spontaneously provide such information to the Tribunal. Furthermore, neither **Article 8 of the Rules**, nor **Article 29 §1 of the Statute** envisage any sanctions applicable to a state that refuses to respond to a request for information issued by the Tribunal. On the other hand, if a country refuses to comply with an official request for referral back, under **Article 11 of the Rules**, *"the court may ask the presiding judge to refer the matter to the Security Council"*.

However, if the international tribunal was not informed in time (i.e. prior to the verdict being handed down by the national instance) the existence of a case being heard by a national jurisdiction (for one of the reasons indicated below) and if it disapproves of the procedures, there is one option open: to re-try the case. However, such an option is governed by strict conditions.

- **Changes to the *non bis in idem* principle**

Article 13 of the Rules of the Tribunal, in accordance with Article 10§1 of the Statute, applies the principle of *non bis in idem*. In effect, it states that, *"If the presiding judge is validly informed that a criminal prosecution is in progress against a person before a national judicial institution for an offence for which the individual has already been tried by the Tribunal, a* *lower court may issue a substantiated order in accordance with the procedure covered under Article 10, mutatis mutandis, inviting the national judicial institution to cease and desist from the prosecution (...)".*

Article 10 §2 of the Statute makes the Tribunal subject to the application of the principle of *non bis in idem*. *"Any person who has been brought before a national jurisdiction for actions constituting serious breaches of international humanitarian law cannot be prosecuted subsequently by an international tribunal (...)"*. However, this article contains changes to the principle because it considers that the Tribunal can decide to try an offender again if *"the offence for which he/she was tried was considered to be a crime under common law; or the national jurisdiction had not judged the case impartially or independently, since the proceedings it instituted were intended to release the accused from his/her international criminal responsibility, or the prosecution was not pursued with due diligence"*. It would appear that, thanks to these changes, the Tribunal is entitled to bypass the *non bis in idem*.

The changes made to this principle might cause objections to be raised as regards their apparent incompatibility with **Article 14 §7 of the International Covenant on Civil and Political Rights,** which states that: *"No one person shall be prosecuted or punished due to an offence of which he or she has already been **acquitted or convicted** by a final judgement in accordance with he law and criminal procedure of each country"*. However, this arrangement certainly did not take into account the creation of an objective and impartial international independent tribunal. And especially as, it should be remember that the application of the *non bis in idem* principle remains strict and inviolate in the case of national jurisdictions. The fair administration of justice lies behind the argument in favour of exceptions to the principle of *non bis in idem*. In fact, the re-trial of a case by the international tribunal would be free of any prejudice, since it could go in favour of the accused just as well as it could go against him or her.

2. COOPERATION FROM THE STATES AND LEGAL AID

"All the States shall fully cooperate with the international Tribunal and its organs, (...) and all the States shall take the necessary measures with regards to their internal right to apply the arrangements of the present resolution and the Statute (...)"[17], in application of **Article 48 of the United National Charter** which requires member States to take *"the action required to carry out the resolutions of the Security Council for the maintenance of international peace and security"*. At the time of writing, only four member States – Italy[18], the Netherlands, Spain and Portugal – have adapted their legislation accordingly. Other countries, including France (the parliamentary session of Autumn, 1994)[19], Norway, Switzerland, Belgium and Germany are currently adopting such measures.

The cooperation between States and the international Tribunal is a fundamental principle behind the smooth operation of such a Tribunal. Without the member States, the goal of ensuring the criminals are brought to justice could never be attained. The choice in Chapter VII of the United Nations Charter as the legal framework for the creation of a Tribunal to judge former Yugoslavia has the theoretical advantage of creating a mechanism which is binding upon countries. But if the effectiveness of legal action by the Tribunal is made possible through such a mechanism, its effectiveness is not guaranteed in practice. One may even wonder what will happen to the sanctions

---

17. See Security Council Resolution 827 §4.

18. For example, as regards Italy, see Decree-Law No. 544 of 28 December, 1993: "Arrangements concerning cooperation with the international Tribunal for the prosecution of serious breaches of international humanitarian law committed on the territory of former Yugoslavia" in the *Gazetta ufficiale della Republica italiana* dated22 February, 1994, General series No. 43.

19. See Appendices.

which the Security Council may implement should there be a refusal to cooperate on the part of any state, especially the countries of Former Yugoslavia (these already having been subjected to numerous condemnations). It is not hardly like to be the fear of suffering some sort of Security Council condemnation which will cause a country to cooperate with the Tribunal. This can only happen if the **political will** is there.

a. Cooperation with the investigation procedure

In concrete terms, and as is emphasised by the Secretary-General in his report, *"all the countries are required to cooperate with the Tribunal and to cooperate **with all the stages of the proceedings,** so that requests for assistance in gathering evidence and the testimony of witnesses, suspects and experts, identification and search for individuals and the despatch of court orders"*[20]. It should be noted here that numerous countries (especially Germany, Austria, Bosnia-Herzegovina, Canada, Croatia, Denmark, United States, France, Norway, Slovenia, Sweden, Switzerland and the Ukraine) having responded to requests contained in Security Council Resolutions 771 (1992) and 780 (1992) as well as the requests from the Commission of Experts for Former Yugoslavia[21] concerning the establishment of proof of serious breaches of international humanitarian law committed on the territory of former Yugoslavia. The various reports thus established by the countries and transmitted to the Commission of experts are currently of such a nature as to facilitate the work of the Prosecutor in his investigation of the various cases.

The duty of cooperation is repeated throughout the internal Rules of the international Tribunal.

---

20. See Chapter 6 Doc. S/25704.
21. For more information, refer to the explanations regarding the Bassiouni Commission.

Thus, under the terms of **Article 8**:when "*a breach committed within the jurisdiction of the Tribunal is the subject or has been the subject of a criminal investigation or prosecution before a national judicial body, [the Tribunal] may ask the state to which this body belongs to provide it with all the relevant information*", in application of Article 29 §1 of the Statute.

Similarly, under **Article 39 of the Rules** concerning the conduct of investigations, i.e., the summonses and questioning of suspects, taking oral evidence from victims, witnesses and recording their statements, the gathering of evidence and on-the-spot investigations, the Prosecutor is competent to "*obtain for these purposes the assistance of all the competent national bodies as well as any international body including the International Organisation of Detective Forces (INTERPOL)*". The practical procedures for cooperation between Interpol an the Tribunal were laid down in Autumn, 1994 during the Annual General Meeting of that organisation (AGM/63/RAP. No. 13, see appendix).

Furthermore, the countries must also implement such court orders as arrest warrants, search warrants, bench warrants or transfer warrants and to put any other court order into practise. **Article 40 of the Rules** entitled "Precautionary Measures" states that, "*In cases of emergency, the Prosecutor may ask any country to proceed to the arrest and remand in custody of a suspect* (the use of the expression "remand in custody" assumes that the countries must grant the suspect all the guarantees covered by remands in their own legislation), *and to seize all material evidence; to take any measure necessary to prevent the escape of a suspect or of an accused, and to prevent the intimidation or infliction of physical harm on victims or witnesses, or the destruction of evidence*".

The cooperation of States rests solely on a legal obligation which has no penalties attached to it and on a "disciplinary procedure" designed to require States to comply with it. However, as regards arrest warrants, bench warrants, transfer warrants and the service of the bill of indictment, there are certain ways of forcing compliance. In fact, according to the Secretary-General's report, a bench warrant or an order to warrant to the custody of the Tribunal issued by the lower court are considered as putting into effect a coercive measure covered by Chapter VII of the United Nations Charter. The punishment provided for is a report to the Security Council from the presiding judge, who officially informs the Council that the States concerned are refusing to cooperate. This type of sanction is also planned if there is a failure to implement an arrest warrant (see **Article 59**) and should there be no service of the bill of indictment, where the bill is "attributable in whole or in part to the default or refusal to cooperate with the Tribunal on the part of a state" (see **Article 61E**).

- **Remarks concerning the cooperation between the Tribunal and other organs of the UN**

The Security Council, in its **resolution 771** of 13 August, 1992, had asked the States and international humanitarian organisations to gather information on the subject of breaches of human rights, including serious breaches of the Geneva Conventions committed on the territory of former Yugoslavia and to place such information at its disposal. There is also the important work performed by Tadeusz Mazowiecki, Special Rapporteur of the Commission on Human Rights.

Similarly, in its **Resolution 780** in 6 October, 1992, he asked the Secretary General to set up an impartial commission of experts[22] responsible for examining and analysing the information collected under **Resolution 771**, in order to supply the Secretary-General with its conclusions concerning serious breaches of the Geneva Conventions and international humanitarian law of which there was proof that these had been committed on the territory of former Yugoslavia.

---

22. Chaired by Cherif Bassiouni.

Thus, **a basic set of information has already been created**, evidence has been collected. So there is a foundation which can be used by the Tribunal.

The information is operational due to the rules of prudence and objectivity which governed its collection. However, it cannot be used by the Tribunal in its raw state; it needs to be investigated thoroughly, the evidence in it needs to be corroborated, each case must be carefully examined, with a view to countering any argument concerning any possible contamination of the information which might be advanced by the defence.

EXTRACT FROM THE BASSIOUNI REPORT[23]

In December, 1992, the Commission set up a database with the intention of creating a complete and usable file concerning all the allegations indicated of serious violations of the Geneva Conventions and other breaches of international humanitarian law committed on the territory of former Yugoslavia (...). The data received came from various governments and were communicated officially, as well from intergovernmental and non-governmental organisations. The database also contained information supplied by organs of the United Nations, as well as information from public sources and from the media.

The database was sent to the Prosecutor's Office of the International Tribunal.

---

23. Cf. Doc. S/1994/674 p. 10.

WHAT IS THE BASSIOUNI COMMISSION?

The Bassiouni Commission is a commission of experts set up by the Secretary-General of the United Nations under §3 of Security Council Resolution 780 (1992). It consists of five experts. It was chaired by Fritz Kalshoven until 19 October, 1993 and then by Cherif Bassiouni. It is responsible for examining and analysing information gathered in the context of resolutions 771 (1992) and 780 (1992) in order to present the Secretary-General with its conclusions concerning the serious breaches of the Geneva Conventions and other breaches of international humanitarian law which could be proved to have been committed in the territory of former Yugoslavia. It was most particularly concerned with investigating the practise of ethnic cleansing.

After the creation of the Tribunal, the Security Council asked the Commission to continue to collect the information it had been required to gather under its terms of reference as a matter of urgency until a Prosecutor was appointed. Its final report was made public in May, 1994 and contained over 3000 pages of additional material (See Doc S/1994/674).

b. Cooperation in carrying out of the sentence

- **Carrying out of the sentence through the intermediary of a state**

WHAT PUNISHMENTS COULD THE ACCUSED EXPECT IF FOUND GUILTY?

- **The International Criminal Tribunal is not able to pronounce the death sentence.**

- **No autonomous sentence is planned for under international law.**

- **In pronouncing sentence, the Tribunal refers to the general scale of terms of imprisonment as applied by the courts of former Yugoslavia.**

The States of former Yugoslavia would not appear to be among those liable to be asked to carry out the sentences. It is important to consolidate the international character of the tribunal, this character having to be constantly reaffirmed in view of the close ties which unite these countries to the crimes perpetrated, their authors and their victims. Thus, **with the exception of the countries of former Yugoslavia, all the member States of the U.N. are candidates for carrying out the sentences**, subject to their respect for rights guaranteed to persons deprived of their liberty, rights which feature in Article 10 of the International Covenant on Civil and Political Rights. The administering state will be designated by the Tribunal on the list of States who have informed the Security Council that they were willing to accepted those convicted of crimes (see **Article 27 of the Statute** of the Tribunal and **Article 103 of the Rules**).

The sentences will be served in accordance with the law and internal procedures of the state in question under the control of the international Tribunal. It should be emphasised that under **Article 24 of the Statute**, the international Tribunal cannot pronounce the death sentence, in accordance with the wishes of the United Nations, as expressed by the General Assembly in Resolution 44/128 of 15 December, 1989.

- **Pardons and commutation of sentence**

Pardons or commutation of sentences are the prerogative of the state administering the sentence. However, **Article 29 of the Statute** and **Chapter 9 of the Rules** do not confer such a right to the state concerned unless it has been authorised in advance by the International Tribunal. It is thus up to the later, through the presiding judge, after consultation with the judges, to decide whether the prisoner could benefit from such measures or not by virtue of the criminal law of the country responsible for carrying out the sentence. This solution thus associates the country responsible for carrying out the sentence with the international Tribunal and confirms the primacy of the latter over national jurisdictions, because it is up to it to decide in the interests of justice and general principles of law. It thus rules within a strictly legal, rather than a political, framework.

- **Compensation for victims**

The Tribunal has not been empowered by the Security Council to rule on the matter of compensation to which victims might be entitled, as a result of the damage caused by the serious breaches of international humanitarian law. This task is the exclusive prerogative of the national courts which are competent under the relevant rules of internal law (see Security Council

Resolution 827 §6). The victim or his/her representatives must therefore institute proceedings before a national jurisdiction in order to obtain reparations for the damage suffered. On this point, the question of the guilt of the perpetrator should not have to be discussed by the national jurisdiction, the Tribunal having already ruled definitively and decisively on this point (see Article 106 of the Rules).

In this respect the Danish Helsinki Committee, in a note entitled "An International Court of Civil Claims" has raised some interesting points. It deals with the risk that national jurisdictions might be choked with a large number of claims and suggests the creation of an international tribunal called upon to rule on civil suits from victims. The establishment of such a court ought to be integrated into the peace treaty which would confirm the end of hostilities.

The procedure would consist of three phases: the first would involve lodging the complaint, gathering the evidence and identifying those persons who were the subject of the complaint. The victims ought to benefit from legal assistance at this stage. The judgement would constitute the second phase of the proceedings. The court could pronounce judgement by default should the defendant be absent. The third and final phase would be the implementation of the resolution. This would assume the effective cooperation of the States of former Yugoslavia, as regards respect for and application of the judgements. If necessary, new penalties could be devised in order to force them to implement these judgements. A reparations fund would be created, funded by frozen assets belonging to the States and held by the court[24] and by frozen capital invested abroad by the criminals.

---

24. The Danish Helsinki Committee is assuming here that the States of former Yugoslavia also have civil responsibility.

The Security Council Resolution (S/RES/687) concerning the situation between Iraq and Kuwait which created a special fund to cover matters concerning the problems of compensation and damages for which Iraq was responsible[25] is also relevant here. However, this proposal would appear to us to be difficult to defend in the special context of former Yugoslavia. In fact, if in the case of the Gulf War, the responsibility could be clearly laid at the door of a particular State, namely Iraq, the Yugoslavian situation is different: the criminals are individuals who are individually criminally responsible.

---

25. A commission was appointed to manage this fund which was supplied with finance by a percentage levy on revenue from Iraqi oil.

II. TRYING THE CRIMINALS: THE RESOURCES ALLOCATED

1. REMANDING THE ACCUSED TO THE CUSTODY OF THE COURT

a. A procedure different from that of standard extradition

"**Extradition.** The surrender by one state to another of a person accused of committing an offence in the latter".[26]

Extradition is not a standard requirement in law, therefore international extradition law is purely contract law. Treaties concluded in this area are in a bilateral or multilateral form and generally have a double purpose, namely, to make extradition possible for countries which, like most of the English-speaking countries make it subject to the existence of treaty, and to create a commitment to extradite under the circumstances and conditions laid down in the text of the treaty.

The treaties thus determine which breaches are subject to extradition, either in making a list or in specifying that an offence punishable by the laws of both parties to the treaty and which in

---

26. A Concise Dictionary of Law, 2nd Edition, Oxford University Press, 1990, p. 162.

both cases would result in a minimum term of imprisonment is an extraditable offence. Furthermore, they determine the conditions which must be fulfilled in order for extradition to be granted or under which it could be granted, for example by requiring dual criminal liability or by excluding extradition for offences which could be described as political.

Article 29 of the Statute of the international Tribunal mentions the **transfer** of an accused from a state to the headquarters of the Tribunal rather than extradition. This is justified by the fact that the question of handing over the accused to the Tribunal arises under different circumstances from those of a classic extradition problem. The requirement to hand over the accused covered by the Statute is the result not of a treaty obligation but of the duty which U.N. member States have to implement the resolutions of the Security Council. Furthermore, this obligation is designed not to benefit another state but an international jurisdiction.

This mechanism makes it possible to short-circuit the problems raised by extradition. The procedures do not have to be followed nor do the basic conditions need to exist which are normally required by national legislation in this respect. Thus a defendant can be transferred to the Tribunal by a state whose laws may normally prohibit extradition of its nationals (see Doc. S/ 25266). In this respect, **Article 58 of the Rules** of the Tribunal, entitled "Provisions of internal law concerning extradition" indicates that, "*The obligations stated in Article 29 of the Statute shall prevail over any legal obstacles which national legislation or extradition treaties to which the state in question is a party might otherwise use to obstruct the transfer of the accused to the Tribunal*".

The idea, according to which the Tribunal could be considered as being a mere extension of the national tribunals of the States may not be foreign to the reasoning which governed the formulation of Article 29 of the Statute. Countries may be induced to combine their jurisdictions in the matter of law enforcement and to entrust this jurisdiction to an international tribunal which would then serve as a joint criminal jurisdiction. This combination could result either from an agreement (it could be said in this respect that the jurisdiction of the international military tribunal of Nuremberg resulted from a similar combination of the national jurisdictions of States which were parties to the London Agreement), or, as is the case here, a Security Council resolution forcing them to do so. It should be noted that the reciprocal limitation of sovereignties resulting therefrom, whether agreed or imposed, is agreed to in the interest of organising a peace, its continuation or its re-establishment.

The result of the above is that the Tribunal thus created **is not a foreign court,** since relations between States are not involved. It is not a state which requires the handing over of an accused but the international community "personified" by the international Tribunal. Consequently, the immediate handover of the accused can be proceeded with without the necessity of initiating an extradition procedure.

The simplified procedure for handing over the accused adopted by the Statute of the Tribunal is an **old idea**. In fact, Article 5 of the draft Convention of the London International Association dated 1943 mentions the creation of an international criminal court and says, *"The handing over of an accused to the prosecution service of the international criminal court is not an extradition. For the purpose of the application of the present Convention, the international criminal court is considered to be a joint criminal jurisdiction common to all nations and the justice rendered by it is not considered as foreign justice".*[27] Similarly, Resolution 3 (I) of the General Assembly dated 13 February, 1946, although it was entitled "Extradition and Punishment of War Criminals" recommended the States to *"take all the*

---

27. History of the problem of international criminal jurisdiction, Memorandum from the Secretary-General, 1949, V,8, Appendix 9B.

necessary measures" to send back to the countries in which the offences were committed *"those responsible for the crimes defined in the London Agreement"* without specifically mentioning extradition among these measures (See doc S.25266).

b. Critique: the absence of true sanctions

WHAT SANCTIONS COULD BE APPLIED TO A COUNTRY WHICH REFUSES TO COOPERATE WITH THIS TRIBUNAL?

* **No automatic sanction has been considered.**

* **A possible sanction is left to the discretion of the Security Council, informed of such non-cooperation by the presiding judge of the Tribunal.**

The procedure described above thus aims at making it easy to hand over to the tribunal those persons who may be accused of serious breaches of international humanitarian law. However, they do not guarantee its effectiveness. In fact, if the bench warrant and the transfer order under guard to the Tribunal are considered to constitute a coercive measure under Chapter VII of the United Nations Charter, what punishment could be inflicted on a state which refuses to hand over a criminal? The only measure covered by the Rules under their Articles 59 and 61, is that the Security Council would be informed by the presiding judge of the refusal of a country to execute an arrest warrant. These provisions do not settle the question of the nature of the punishment which could be imposed by the Security Council. Could one reasonably consider the imposition of an economic embargo, resolved by the international community as a whole and applied to an offending state, even if it is not a major economic world power?

The problem of the absence of genuine sanctions is particularly important with respect to those countries which are parties to the conflict in former Yugoslavia. In fact, as we have already emphasised, the state of the institutions in some of the countries involved and the war situation which prevails in their territory makes it most unlikely that prosecutions would be effective and thus the principle of *aut dedere, aut judicare*, the only principle offering a minimum guarantee as concerns the prosecution of the perpetrators of serious breaches of international humanitarian law, would also fail to be applied. Furthermore, one could question the nature of the kind of sanctions which would really be effective in this context. Could one envisage, for example, the breaking off of diplomatic relations with one of these countries while peace negotiations were still in progress?

Thus the Tribunal might find it impossible to obtain a handover of the accused and his/her consequent court appearance due, for example, to a lack of political will in this respect.

2. ABSENCE OF THE ACCUSED: AN OBSTACLE TO PROSECUTION AND CONVICTION?

The failure of an accused to make a court appearance would give rise to two questions, one concerning the investigation phase the other concerning the progress of the trial:

- May a person against whom there are serious assumptions regarding the commission of a crime but whom it has not proved possible to apprehend be **tried**, or at the very least **questioned by the police**?
- May an accused who has been convicted of serious breaches of international humanitarian law, but who has **escaped**, be **tried**?

a. The presence of the accused: a basic principle

This principle is laid down in the Statute and the Regulations of the Tribunal. In fact, under **Article 21-4-d of the Statute** concerning the rights of the accused, any person against whom an accusation is made in law, is fully entitled *"to be present during the trial and to defend himself/herself or to have the assistance of a defence counsel of his/her choice"*. This provision is a mere repetition of that contained in Article 14-3-d of the 1966 International Covenant on Civil and Political Rights. The Rules also confirm this principle in **Article 88-(A)** which stipulates that *"the judgement has been pronounced at a public hearing and in the presence of the accused (...)"* as well as in its **Article 101-(D)** which states that *"the sentence is pronounced at a public hearing and in the presence of the person recognised as the guilty party (...)"*.

b. First situation: the absence of the accused from the investigation phase

Article 61-(C) considers that in case of **non-performance of an arrest warrant** (and thus the failure to inform the person named in the indictment either because he/she cannot be found or because he/she is to be found in a country which refuses to hand him/her over), and if the lower court considers *"that there are sufficient reasons to believe that the accused has committed one or all of the offences with which he/she is charged in the indictment, it shall rule in consequence (...)"*. This last expression signifies that the court publicly notes the existence of serious allegations and conclusive proof against the person concerned. The decision pronounced by the court is not a judgement it is merely a **reconfirmation by the panel of judges of the bill of indictment** as a result of which an international arrest warrant would be issued regarding the person in question.

Thus, at this stage in the proceedings the absence of the accused is an obstacle to the opening of the trial and thus to the judgement, but it does not prevent the implementation of international prosecution of the case.

c. Second situation: absence of the accused during the trial

As has already been emphasised, Articles 88 and 101 of the Rules lay down the principle of the accused being present.

However, **Article 102-(B)** concerning the status of a person convicted by the lower court states that, "*if, in accordance with a prior decision by the court, the convicted person is out on bail, or **has been released for any other reason, and is not present at the moment the verdict is pronounced,** the court shall issue a warrant for his/her arrest (...)*". Similarly, **Article 118-(B)** concerning the status of the accused after the appeal judgement has been pronounced (i.e. in the higher court) states that, "*if the accused is **not present on the day the appeal judgement is handed down**, either because he/she was acquitted by the lower court, or because of an order issued in accordance with Article 65 (concerning the granting of bail) **or for any other reason,** the appeal court may pronounce its decision in his/her absence and order his/her arrest and his/her being placed at the disposal of the court, except in the case of an acquittal*". The term "for any other reason" contained in these articles indicates that the accused absconded after arrest and transfer to the headquarters of the Tribunal.

It thus emerges that if the absence of the accused occurs **after** the case has been opened, it can be tried.

These provisions conform to the terms of Article 14.3 of the International Covenant on Civil and Political Rights because they presuppose that no trial can be opened before the accused in physically present before the international Tribunal. Similarly, the possibility for the Tribunal to pronounce judgement and sentence in the absence of the accused does not contravene Article 14.3 of the International Covenant on Civil and Political Rights. This article confers a **right** upon the accused, that of being present at his/her trial and at the pronouncement of the verdict. But if the defendant chooses not to avail himself/herself of this right, by deliberately removing himself/herself from the court, this absence shall not interfere with the conduct of the trial.

If Article 14 constitutes a legal guarantee for the accused, it must not constitute a guarantee of impunity for the criminals. Furthermore, these arrangements conform to the spirit of the Statute of the Tribunal, the aim of which is to enable criminals to be brought to justice.

Furthermore, a judgement pronounced in the absence of the accused under the conditions defined above is considered to be in the presence of the parties since the Rules do not prevent his/her lawyer from representing him/her. The judgement being considered to be in the presence of the parties stems from the fact that when the accused was arrested *"he/she was notified of the declaration of guilt and the sentence, after which procedures were followed in accordance with Article 103 hereunder"*[28] (Article 102-(B) of the Rules), without it being necessary to re-try him/her.

It would thus appear that all these provisions respect the rights of the defence.

3. A PENAL RESPONSIBILITY THAT WOULD BE DIFFICULT TO DISPUTE

A person convicted of serious violations of international humanitarian law would find it difficult to evade criminal responsibility. In fact the opportunities for taking justifiable excuses, justification or mitigating circumstances into account are limited.

---

28. The condemned person is then taken to the place of detention *"as soon as possible after the expiry of the period allowed for appeal"*.

a. The excuse of official duties

Article 7 of the Statute of the Nuremberg Tribunal states, *"The official post of those accused persons, either as heads of state, or as senior officials, shall not be considered either as a justifiable excuse nor as grounds for reducing the sentence"*. This principle is repeated in **Article 7 §2 of the Statute** of the Tribunal for Former Yugoslavia.

Consequently, **"the Act of State"** does not exist. Furthermore, in the case of the leadership, the fact that any of the incriminating acts listed in the Statute were committed by a subordinate does not absolve them from criminal responsibility they are individually responsible for any crime committed by any of their subordinates, if they were aware of or were in possession of information from which, under the circumstances, they could have deduced that this subordinate was in the process of or on the point of committing such an act, and if they did not take every measure of which they were capable to prevent such an act or to punish the guilty party. In fact, the military high command is held especially liable, as regards members of the armed forces under their authority or other persons under their control, to prevent, and if necessary, reprimand criminal activities and to inform the competent authorities thereof. Thus, even if they did not issue the illegal order to commit a crime, senior officers may be held responsible for crimes committed by their subordinates. This responsibility can be justified as negligence displayed by a senior officer, and as long as such an officer cannot prove his ignorance of the existence of any criminal intent or crime committed by a subordinate, he/she can be prosecuted.

b. The excuse of obeying orders

A subordinate who shall have executed an order from a superior or shall have acted upon an instruction from the government and by doing so shall have committed any of the crimes listed in the Statute of the Tribunal may not invoke the excuse known as **"only obeying orders from above"** and may not claim that he/she cannot be held criminally responsible for an act which he/she was ordered to commit. This is the attitude adopted by **Article 7 §4 of the Statute** of the international tribunal.

However, if the performance of a manifestly illegal order does not in itself constitute a justification, it can be considered as an **extenuating circumstance.** One should consider here the case in which the authority of a superior shall be such that it shall have made it impossible for the subordinate to have any freedom of evaluation or of action. On the contrary, if a moral choice was open to the perpetrator, in no case can the fact of having obeyed an order constitute an extenuating circumstance. In order to know if an extenuating circumstance existed, several factors have to be taken into consideration, such as, for example, the more or less close relationship between a superior officer and his/her subordinate, the perpetrator, the relative precision of the instructions, the presence of absence of the commander at the moment when the order was carried out, the odious nature of the acts ordered to be committed, or, conversely, the possible doubt as regards their illegality.

CONCLUSION

The Yugoslav tragedy and more recently, the genocide committed in Rwanda, pose very serious questions to the international community.

Stimulated by public opinion which is becoming increasingly scandalised and indignant at the apparently immunity from prosecution of the perpetrators of crimes committed in former Yugoslavia, the members of the U.N. Security Council have taken a major initiative in setting up an international criminal Tribunal to try war crimes committed in the territory of former Yugoslavia.

There has been much exhortation in the press and elsewhere to ensure that this Tribunal is not used as an alibi by the international community in an attempt to justify its passivity, and even impotence, in the face of the ethnic cleansing operations.

It should be realised that, even though it is essential to support and promote the activity of this Tribunal, there remains the fact that the ambiguous circumstances in which it was created. The equivocation which may well dog its operation and more generally the painful legal compromises which have been invented are truly an original sin. One must therefore approach this whole enterprise with caution.

It should first be realised that the Tribunal was instituted by virtue of Chapter VII of the United Nations Charter and consequently its basic raison d'être is to work to restore peace.

In other words, as soon as the restoration of peace becomes dependent upon a negotiating process that becomes bogged down, and in which cynicism is frequently the order of the day, it is important to be on the alert for the moment to be decided by the international community to put an end to the work of the Tribunal on the pretext of restoring peace for good within the territory of former Yugoslavia. Yet it is common knowledge that the re-establishment of peace would result from partially secret agreements and negotiations, without the peoples involved being able to exercise full control over the said agreements.

The second major ambiguity is the result of the pursuit of the negotiating process, at the same time as the work of the Tribunal is in progress. The negotiations are being sought with, among others, the Bosnian Serb leaders whose numbers include those who were designated 18 months ago as the architects of the ethnic cleansing operations.

It is hard to imagine that these leaders would fail to use these negotiations in order to secretly obtain, if not extort, a sort of "de facto amnesty" granted by the international community, constituting a sort of guarantee that at no time would they be subject to arrest. This would be in total contradiction to their identification with the principal architects of the genocide perpetrated in Bosnia, in particular.

This de facto amnesty is all the more probable in view of the manner in which negotiations are proceeding, a manner which is to the detriment of the international community, in view of its inability to have prevented the Serbs from presenting themselves in a position of strength, in view of their territorial gains which are largely irreversible.

Since the Serbs, and especially the Bosnian Serbs have been able to flagrantly violate international law with impunity, why should they worry about continuing to do so and thus assume total immunity from retribution?

The examination which this book has made of the internal Rules and the judicial instruments used by the international War Crimes Tribunal for former Yugoslavia shows that each time, a more or less painful compromise was found between the Anglo-Saxon legal system on the one hand and the French system on the other, between the need to be able to identify, arrest and try those persons who by definition are currently staying or are about to stay sheltered on their own soil, the last sanctuary remaining to them, and the respect for the principles of international criminal law.

In other words – and this appears to be its first achievement – the international court's activity risks sentencing a certain number of executions *ad vitam eternam* to stay confined to their Bosnian Serb villages, where they are sheltered from international arrest warrants, always supposing that such warrants will ever be issued.

The abandonment of the procedure of trial *in absentia*, a procedure which is rather in the French legal tradition, shows if there were a need to do so, the difficulty of finding a balance between the need to fight against immunity from prosecution and the need to respect the principles of a fair trial.

The manner in which the international Tribunal appears to be organised to punish cases of rape and sexual violence also constitutes a spectacular illustration of this difficulty of employing suitable instruments which are properly adapted to the situation, and especially the situation in the field.

Since in the event, time is on the side of the criminals rather than the victims, the examining magistrates and prosecutor at the Hague are in danger of finding themselves in the middle of a legal impasse if they try to enforce the law regarding this kind of offence while attempting to gather incontrovertible evidence and the necessary proof needed to make their efforts credible.

At the time of writing, in the autumn of 1994, the international criminal court has just begun to tackle the task, despite the fact that a certain number of declarations made in the second quarter of 1994 raised the hope of swifter action. Nevertheless, the first trials are due to start in December, 1994.

If the Tribunal has not yet delivered a judgement, the possibility is already being discussed exceptionally of the international community granting the Tribunal the right to extend its jurisdiction to acts of genocide committed in Rwanda.

Such an extension might be considered to be attractive and encouraging, as the first steps towards the establishment of a permanent international criminal court. Such a court has been demanded by international organisations and the International Federation of Human Rights Organisations has done so for decades.

Yet such an extension also represents a danger, in that it could constitute the occasion for the Security Council member States to forget the real need for the Tribunal, in their eagerness to pursue the much easier enforcement, technically and politically, represented by prosecutions of Rwandan leaders. They might abandon all attempts to punish the real architects of the so-called "ethnic cleansing" operations in former Yugoslavia.

There is also a risk that the countries of the South, and especially those of Africa, might see in the Tribunal a sort of "judicial neo-colonialism". That is why the voices being raised here and there demanding that a process be begun which would terminate in the constitution of a Tribunal in Kigali, under international control and administered by international experts, are rather worrying.

These proposals could be extrapolated into the possibility of organising an international structure, perhaps in the near future, which would make it possible for a certain number of countries to request technical or legal assistance to deal locally with serious issues raised by immunity from punishment. Why not, for instance, constitute a sort of **judicial flying squad, available to the UN,** which could intervene in a particular national criminal jurisdiction to guarantee its impartial functioning.

In other words, the response of the international community to universal crimes would not necessarily involve the establishment of *ad hoc* international tribunals, nor by the constitution of a permanent criminal court, a court which would be extremely cumbersome in its procedures and whose independence of operation would not necessarily be guaranteed. It could consist of interventions on a case by case basis, depending on the interests of governments.

International and civil society as a whole ought to be preoccupied with the need to give the new institutions to be created guarantees of absolute political independence, rather than the creation of an institution with a permanent status.

Whatever happens, the Hague Tribunal must and can operate effectively.

The court has judges who are currently competent for the job they are doing now and will be doing tomorrow. It looks likely, and it is to be hoped, that should the Tribunal become bogged down in procedures the most capable of its judges will know how to disentangle it and set it on its true course again.

The Tribunal is capable of dispensing the justice which is capable of ending immunity from prosecution, and this is a condition *sine qua non* of a return to a lasting peace. This also constitutes an essential stage towards tomorrow, and the creation, it should be hoped, of a permanent international criminal court.[29]

---

29. Address of the Tribunal for Former Yugoslavia:
    International Tribunal for Former Yugoslavia
    Churchillplein, 1, P.O. Box 13888
    2501 EW The Hague, The Netherlands
    Tel: (31) 70-344-5347
    Fax: (31) 70-344-5345 or 5343.

SUMMARY
BIBLIOGRAPHY

I. Books

BISERKO, Sonja. *Yugoslavia Collapse War Crimes*, Belgrade, Centre for Anti-War Action, Belgrade Circle, 1993. 274pp.

Code de Procédure Pénale, Paris, Dalloz, 1994

LESCURE, Karine. *Le tribunal pénal international pour l'ex Yougoslavie*, Paris, collection CEDIN, Etudes internationales, Montchrestien, 1994, 303 p.

Nouveau code pénal, Paris, Dalloz, 1994

Nouvel Observateur et Reporters sans Frontières, *Le livre noir de l'ex-Yougoslavie: Purification ethnique et crimes de guerre.* Paris Arléa, 1993, 485 p.

2. Articles

CASTILLO, Maria. "La compétence du tribunal pénal pour la Yougoslavie", RGDIP, 1994. No. 1, pp 61-87.

Conference on Practical Concerns Relating to the Work of the ad hoc Tribunal for the Former Yugoslavia, Brussels, Centre for Anti-War Action. 3 and 4 March, 1994.

Dr. JAKOULJEVIC, Bosko. *Validity of Indictments Brought under Articles 2-2 of the Statute: ad hoc Tribunal for the Former Yugoslavia*, Belgrade, 1994.

Dr. JOSIPOVIC, Ivo. *International Tribunal for War Crimes Committed in the Territory of Former Yugoslavia* (Notes to the Security Council Resolution 827/93) Zagreb 1994.

Dr. OBRADOVIC, Konstantin. *The International Criminal Tribunal for the Former Yugoslavia. Responsibilities of the National Authorities of the Former Yugoslavia for Prosecuting Grave Breaches of International Humanitarian Law: Parallel or Alternative Process to that of the International Tribunal*. Belgrade, 1994.

Dr. SAHOVIC, Milan. *The International Criminal Tribunal for the Former Yugoslavia and the UN Embargo*. Belgrade, 1994.

European Parliament for Foreign Affairs and Security. *Draft Resolution on the Creaion of an International Criminal Tribunal*. Submitted by the Rapporteur, Alexander LANGER (Green Party, Italy).

PELLET, Alain. "Le Tribunal criminel international pour l'ex-Yougoslavie: Poudre aux yeux ou avancée décisive?" RGDIP 1994, No. 1, p 7-60.

SIESBY, Erik. *An International Court of Civil Claims Arising from Criminal Acts Committed during the War in the Former Yugoslavia*. The Danish Helsinki Committee.

Verona Forum for Peace and Reconciliation on the Territory of Former Yugoslavia. *Civic Conference for Peace and Reconciliation on the Territory of Former Yugoslaiva: Are Peace and Democracy Possible under Imposed Ethnic Homogeneity?* Vienna Declaration, 12.06.1993.

3. United Nations Documents

RESOLUTIONS:

S/Res 808 (1993) of 22 February, 1993.

S/Res 827 (1993) of 25 May, 1993.

DOCUMENTS

Fifth report by Tadeusz Masowiecki, Special Rapporteur of the U.N. Commission on Human Rights, Doc E/CN.4/1993/50 of 17 November, 1993.

Committee of French Lawyers. *Rapport sur la création d'un tribunal pénal international appelé à juger des crimes commis dans l'ex-Yougoslavie.* Doc S/25266.

History of the problem of international criminal jurisdiction. Memorandum from the Secretary-general, 1949,V, 8.

Amendment to article 96(ii) of the Rules of Procedure and Evidence, Doc IT/53/Rev.2 dated 5 May, 1994.

Secretary-general's report prepared in accordance with paragraph 2 of Security Council Resolution 808 (1993), Doc S/25704 of 3 May, 1993.

Final report of the Committee of Experts established in accordance with Security Council Resolution 780 (1992), Doc S/1994/674 of 27 May, 1994.

Rules of Procedure and Evidence, adopted on 11 February, 1994, Doc IT/32 of 14 March, 1994.

Rules covering the treatment of persons in custody awaiting trial or appeal before the court or held on order of the court, adopted 5 May, 1994. Doc IT/38/Rev.3 of 10 May, 1994.

4. Interviews[30]

Geneva, Palais des Nations Unies, 14 April, 1994.

Cherif BASSIOUNI, Chair of the Commitee of Experts set up under the terms of Security Council Resolution 780 (1992).

Graham T. BLEWITT, Acting Deputy Prosecutor.

Ralph ZACKLIN, Director and deputy to Deputy Secretary-general, U.N. Bureau of Legal Affairs.

Mr. WIERUZEWSKI, Information Coordinator to the Special Rapporteur, Tadeusz Masowiecki.

The Hague, headquarters of the International Criminal Court for Former Yugoslavia, 26 April, 1994.

Antonio CASSESE, Presiding judge.

Theo VAN BOEVEN, Registrar.

Dominique WOUTERS, Legal adviser.

Paris, Ministry of Justice, 10 May, 1994.

Marianne CHAPELLE, Chargé de Mission of the Criminal Affairs Department.

Paris, 17 May, 1994.

Claude JORDA, French judge at the International Criminal Court for Former Yugoslavia.

Paris, 9 June, 1994.

Mireille DELMAS-MARTY, Professor of Criminal Law at the University of Paris I Panthéon-Sorbonne.

---

30. We thank all those who agreed to talk to us.

ORGANIZATIONS WHICH TOOK
THE INITIATIVE TO PRODUCE
THIS BOOK

A UNIVERSITY PARTNER:

CEDIN

AN NGO FOR THE PROTECTION OF
HUMAN RIGHTS

FIDH

A HUMANITARIAN NGO:

MSF

CEDIN

CEDIN was created in 1981 as part of the University of Paris X Nanterre with three major objectives in mind:
- to contribute to the expansion **of research and consideration of international law, in a constant relationship with legal practice** and world events.
- to promote the **teaching of research techniques** to post-graduate students, through their direct participation in the work of the Centre, jointly with all those involved in teaching international law with whom they are closely associated.
- to constitute **an open meeting-place for teachers, lecturers and practitioners,** both French and foreign, through exchanges and joint research projects, thus contributing to the enhancement of international law studies, both under the aegis of the university and outside it.

As its activities expanded, CEDIN decided in 1992 that, while remaining faithful to its initial purpose, it should adopt a new structure, under the federative title of **Centre for International Law**, and establish three joint research centres:
- CEDIN-Paris I, under the direction of Brigitte STERN, who was one of the main compilers of this book.
- CEDIX-Paris X Nanterre, co-directed by Emmanuel DECAUX and Alain PELLET.
- CEDIN -Paris XIII, directed by Pierre-Michel EISEMANN.

These three units are institutional members of the Committee for the Compilation of the French International Law Yearbook published by the CNRS.

CEDIN-Paris I:
9 rue Mahler, 75004 Paris

FIDH

The International Federation of Human Rights Leagues, FIDH, is an international non-governmental organisation concerned with the universal defence of human rights. It was created in 1922, and now has nearly 90 affiliates throughout the world.

The FIDH is accredited to the United Nations Organisation, UNESCO, the Council of Europe and the Organisation for African Unity.

In the last 10 years, the FIDH has conducted nearly one thousand missions of investigation, judicial inquiry, mediation or training in about 100 countries.

The FIDH also acts as a service-provider to its members in the fields of legal and judicial cooperation or in acting as their representative in dealings with intergovernmental organisations.

The FIDH is also proactive in attempting to ensure that international law develops in such a way as to ensure effective protection for human rights.

The FIDH is headquartered in Paris, with offices in Geneva, New York, Brussels and Stockholm.

INTERNATIONAL FEDERATION OF HUMAN RIGHTS LEAGUES (FEDERATION INTERNATIONALE DES LIGUES DES DROITS DE L'HOMME)
14 Passage de la Main d'Or, 75011 Paris, France

MSF

Médecins sans Frontières, MSF, is a humanitarian association of a medical nature, created in France in 1971.

Today, with its international network, it can claim to be the world's leading private humanitarian aid organisation.

Médecins sans Frontières, in all its branches, sends a total of more than 2000 volunteers out into the field.

MSF was created as a major departure from the methods of the International Red Cross, and can claim today to have a very special relationship with international humanitarian law. MSF does not seek to defend an international right of intervention but makes itself the advocate of the rights of victims to aid, respect and dignity.

An integral part of the MSF's mission, and equal in importance to action in the field, is the collection of evidence relating to two different types of intervention – information and accusation.

MSF
MEDECINS SANS FRONTIERES
8 rue Saint-Sabin, 75011 Paris

APPENDICES

- Security Council Resolution 808 (22 February, 1993).
- Security Council Resolution 827 (25 May, 1993).
- Rules of procedure and evidence of the Hague Tribunal (as amended 6 October 1995)

UNITED NATIONS

SECURITY COUNCIL/178
22 FEBRUARY 1993

Resolution (S/25314)

The Security Council,

Reaffirming its resolution 713 (1991) of 25 September 1991 and all subsequent resolutions,

Recalling paragraph 10 of its resolutions 764 (1992) of 13 July 1992, in which it reaffirmed that all parties are bound to comply with the obligations under international humanitarian law, in particular the Geneva Conventions of 12 August 1949, and that persons who commit or order the commission of grave breaches of the Conventions are individually responsible in respect of such breaches,

Recalling also its resolution 771 (1992) of 13 August 1992, in which *inter alia,* it demanded that all parties and others concerned in the former Yugoslavia, and all military forces in Bosnia and Herzegovina, immediately cease and desist from all breaches of international humanitarian law,

Recalling further its resolution 780 (1992) of 6 October 1992, in which it requested the Secretary-General to establish, as a matter of urgency, an impartial commission of experts to examine and analyse the information submitted pursuant to resolutions 771 (1992) and 780 (1992), together with such further information as the commission may obtain, with a view to providing the Secretary-General with its conclusions on the evidence of grave breaches of the Geneva Conventions and other violations of international humanitarian law committed in the territory of the former Yugoslavia,

Having considered the interim report of the Commission of Experts established pursuant to resolution 780 (1992) (S/25274), in which the Commission observed that a decision to establish an ad hoc international tribunal in relation to events in the territory of the former Yugoslavia would be consistent with the direction of the work,

Expressing once again its *grave alarm* at continuing reports of widespread violations of international humanitarian law occurring within the territory of the former Yugoslavia, including reports of mass killings and the continuance of the practice of "ethnic cleansing",

Determining that this situation constitutes a threat to international peace and security,

Determined to put an end to such crimes and to take effective measures to bring to justice the persons who are responsible for them,

Convinced that in the particular circumstances of the former Yugoslavia the establishment of an international tribunal would enable this aim to be achieved and would contribute to the restoration and maintenance of peace,

Noting in this regard the recommendation by the Co-Chairmen of the Steering Committee of the International Conference on the Former Yugoslavia for the establishment of such a tribunal (S/25221),

Taking note with grave concern of the report of the European Community investigative mission into the treatment of Muslim women in the Former Yugoslavia, (S/25240, Annex I),

Taking note of the report of the committee of jurists submitted by France (S/25266), the report of the commission of jurists submitted by Italy, (S/25300) and the report transmitted by the Permanent Representative of Sweden on behalf of the Chairman-in-Office of the Conference on Security and Cooperation in Europe (S/25307),

1. *Decides* that an international tribunal shall be established for the prosecution of persons responsible for serious violations of

international humanitarian law committed in the territory of the Former Yugoslavia since 1991,

2. *Requests* the Secretary-General to submit for consideration by the Council at the earliest possible date, and if possible no later than sixty days after the adoption of the present resolution, a report on all aspects of this matter, including specific proposals and where appropriate options for the effective and expeditious implementation of the decision contained in paragraph 1 above, taking into account suggestions put forward in this regard by Member States;

3. *Decides* to remain actively seized of the matter.

UNITED NATIONS

SECURITY COUNCIL
S/RES/827 (1993)
25 MAY 1993

Resolution 827 (1993)

Adopted by the Security Council at the 3217 meeting, 25 May 1993,

The Security Council,

Reaffirming its resolutions 713 (1991) of 25 September 1991 and all subsequent relevant resolutions,

Having considered the report of the Secretary-General of 3 and 17 May 1993 pursuant to paragraph 2 of resolution 808 (1993),

Expressing once again its grave alarm at continuing reports of widespread and flagrant violations of international humanitarian law occurring within the territory of the former Yugoslavia, and especially in the Republic of Bosnia and Herzegovina, including reports of mass killings, massive, organized and systematic detention and rape of women and the continuance of the practice of "ethnic cleansing", including for the acquisition and the holding of territory,

Determining that this situation continues to constitute a threat to international peace and security.

Determined to put an end to such crimes and to take effective measures to bring to justice the persons who are responsible for them,

Convinced that in the particular circumstances of the former Yugoslavia the establishment as an ad hoc measure by the Council of an international tribunal and the prosecution of persons responsible for serious violations of international humanitarian law would enable this aim to be achieved and would contribute to the restoration and maintenance of peace,

Believing that the establishment of an international tribunal and the prosecution of persons responsible for the above-mentioned violations of international humanitarian law will contribute to ensuring that such violations are halted and effectively redressed,

Noting in this regard the recommendation by the Co-Chairmen of the Steering Committee of the International Conference on the Former Yugoslavia for the establishment of such a tribunal,

Reaffirming in this regard its decision in resolution 808 (1993) of 22 February 1993 that an international tribunal shall be established for the prosecution of persons responsible for serious violations of international humanitarian law committed in the territory of the former Yugoslavia since 1991,

Considering that, pending the appointment of the prosecutor of the international tribunal, the Commission of Experts established pursuant to resolution 780 (1992) should continue on an urgent basis the collection of information relating to evidence of grave breaches of the Geneva Conventions and other violations of international humanitarian law as proposed in its interim report,

Acting under Chapter VII of the Charter of the United Nations,

1. *Approves* the report of the Secretary-General;

2. *Decides* hereby to establish an international tribunal for the sole purpose of prosecuting persons responsible for serious violations of international humanitarian law committed in the territory of the former Yugoslavia between 1 January 1991 and a date to be determined by the Security Council upon the restoration of peace and to this end to adopt the statute of the International Tribunal annexed to the report of the Secretary-General;

3. *Requests* the Secretary-General to submit to the judges of the International Tribunal, upon their election, any suggestions received from the States for the rules of procedure and evidence called for under Article 15 of the Statute of the International Tribunal;

4. *Decides* that all the States shall co-operate fully with the International Tribunal and its organs in accordance with the present resolution and the Statute of the International Tribunal and that consequently all States shall take any measures necessary under their domestic law to implement the proviso of the present resolution and the Statute, including the obligation of States to comply with requests for assistance or orders issued by a Trial Chamber under Article 29 of the Statute;

5. *Urges* States and intergovernmental and non-governmental organisations to contribute funds, equipment and services to the International Tribunal, including the offer of expert personnel;

6. *Decides* that the determination of the seat of the International Tribunal is subject to the conclusion of appropriate arrangements between the United Nations and the Netherlands acceptable to the Council, and that the International Tribunal may sit elsewhere when it considers it necessary for the efficient exercise of its functions;

7. *Decides also* that the work of the International Tribunal shall be carried out without prejudice to the right of the victims to seek, through appropriate means, compensation for damages incurred as a result of violations of international humanitarian law;

8. *Requests* the Secretary-General to implement urgently the present resolution and in particular to make practical arrangements for the effective functioning of the International Tribunal at the earliest time and to report periodically to the Council;

9. *Decides* to remain actively seized of the matter.

UNITED
NATIONS

International Tribunal for the
Prosecution of Persons
Responsible for Serious Violations
of International Humanitarian Law
Committed in the Territory of
Former Yugoslavia since 1991

IT/32/Rev. 6

6 October 1995

Original:
English & French

Eighth Session
The Hague
The Netherlands
4 - 6 October 1995

RULES OF PROCEDURE AND EVIDENCE

(ADOPTED ON 11 FEBRUARY 1994)

(AS AMENDED 5 MAY 1994)

(AS FURTHER AMENDED 4 OCTOBER 1994)

(AS REVISED 30 JANUARY 1995)

(AS AMENDED 3 MAY 1995)

(AS FURTHER AMENDED 15 JUNE 1995)

(AS AMENDED 6 OCTOBER 1995)

CONTENTS

PART   **Page**

One   GENERAL PROVISIONS 1

        Rule 1   Entry into Force 1

        Rule 2   Definitions 1

        Rule 3   Languages 3

        Rule 4   Meetings away from the Seat of the Tribunal 4

        Rule 5   Non-compliance with Rules 4

        Rule 6   Amendment of the Rules 5

        Rule 7   Authentic Texts 5

Two   PRIMACY OF THE TRIBUNAL 6

        Rule 8   Request for Information 6

        Rule 9   Prosecutor's Request for Deferral 6

        Rule 10   Formal Request for Deferral 7

        Rule 11   Non-compliance with a Request for Deferral 8

        Rule 12   Determinations of Courts of any State 8

        Rule 13   Non Bis in Idem 8

Three ORGANIZATION OF THE TRIBUNAL 9

        Section 1   The Judges 9

        Rule 14   Solemn Declaration 9

        Rule 15   Disqualification of Judges 9

        Rule 16   Resignation 10

        Rule 17   Precedence 11

        Section 2   The Presidency 11

        Rule 18   Election of the President 11

        Rule 19   Functions of the President 12

        Rule 20   The Vice-President 12

Rule 21   Functions of the Vice-President 13

Rule 22   Replacements 13

Section 3   Internal Functioning of the Tribunal 13

Rule 23   The Bureau 13

Rule 24   Plenary Meetings of the Tribunal 14

Rule 25   Dates of Plenary Sessions 14

Rule 26   Quorum and Vote 15

Section 4   The Chambers 15

Rule 27   Rotation 15

Rule 28   Assignment to Review Indictments 16

Rule 29   Deliberations 16

Section 5   The Registry 16

Rule 30   Appointment of the Registrar 16

Rule 31   Appointment of the Deputy Registrar and the

             Registry Staff 16

Rule 32   Solemn Declaration 17

Rule 33   Functions of the Registrar 17

Rule 34   Victims and Witnesses Unit 18

Rule 35   Minutes 18

Rule 36   Record Book 18

Section 6   The Prosecutor 19

Rule 37   Functions of the Prosecutor 19

Rule 38   Deputy Prosecutor 19

Four   INVESTIGATIONS AND RIGHTS OF SUSPECTS 20

        Section 1   Investigations 20

        Rule 39   Conduct of Investigations 20
        Rule 40   Provisional Measures 21
        Rule 41   Retention of Information 21
        Rule 42   Rights of Suspects during Investigation 21
        Rule 43   Recording Questioning of Suspects 22

        Section 2   Of Counsel 23

        Rule 44   Appointment and Qualifications of Counsel 23
        Rule 45   Assignment of Counsel 24
        Rule 46   Misconduct of Counsel 25

Five   PRE-TRIAL PROCEEDINGS 26

        Section 1   Indictments 26

        Rule 47   Submission of Indictment by the Prosecutor 26
        Rule 48   Joinder of Accused 27
        Rule 49   Joinder of Crimes 27
        Rule 50   Amendment of Indictment 27
        Rule 51   Withdrawal of Indictment 27
        Rule 52   Public Character of Indictment 28
        Rule 53   Non-disclosure of Indictment 28

        Section 2   Orders and Warrants 29

        Rule 54   General Rule 29
        Rule 55   Execution of Arrest Warrants 29
        Rule 56   Cooperation of States 30
        Rule 57   Procedure after Arrest 30
        Rule 58   National Extradition Provisions 30

Rule 59   Failure to Execute a Warrant or Transfer Order 31

Rule 60   Advertisement of Indictment 31

Rule 61   Procedure in Case of Failure to Execute a Warrant ..31

Rule 62   Initial Appearance of Accused 33

Rule 63   Questioning of Accused 34

Rule 64   Detention on Remand 34

Rule 65   Provisional Release 34

Section 3   Production of Evidence 35

Rule 66   Disclosure by the Prosecutor 35

Rule 67   Reciprocal Disclosure 36

Rule 68   Disclosure of Exculpatory Evidence 37

Rule 69   Protection of Victims and Witnesses 38

Rule 70   Matters not Subject to Disclosure 38

Section 4   Depositions 40

Rule 71   Depositions 40

Section 5   Preliminary Motions 41

Rule 72   General Provisions 41

Rule 73   Preliminary Motions by Accused 41

Six   PROCEEDINGS BEFORE TRIAL CHAMBERS 43

Section 1   General Provisions 43

Rule 74   Amicus Curiae 43

Rule 75   Measures for the Protection of Victims and

           Witnesses 43

Rule 76   Solemn Declaration by Interpreters

           and Translators 44

Rule 77   Contempt of the Tribunal 45

Rule 78   Open Sessions 45

Rule 79   Closed Sessions 46

Rule 80   Control of Proceedings 46

Rule 81   Records of Proceedings and Evidence 47

Section 2   Case Presentation 47

Rule 82   Joint and Separate Trials 47

Rule 83   Instruments of Restraint 48

Rule 84   Opening Statements 48

Rule 85   Presentation of Evidence 48

Rule 86   Closing Arguments 49

Rule 87   Deliberations 49

Rule 88   Judgement 50

Section 3   Rules of Evidence 51

Rule 89   General Provisions 51

Rule 90   Testimony of Witnesses 52

Rule 90 bis Transfer of a Detained Witness 53

Rule 91   False Testimony under Solemn Declaration 54

Rule 92   Confessions 55

Rule 93   Evidence of Consistent Pattern of Conduct 55

Rule 94   Judicial Notice 55

Rule 95   Evidence Obtained by Means Contrary to
             Internationally Protected Human Rights 56

Rule 96   Evidence in Cases of Sexual Assault 56

Rule 97   Lawyer-Client Privilege 57

Rule 98   Power of Chambers to Order Production of
             Additional Evidence 57

Section 4   Sentencing Procedure 58

Rule 99   Status of the Acquitted Person 58

Rule 100   Pre-sentencing Procedure 58

Rule 101   Penalties 58

Rule 102   Status of the Convicted Person 60

Rule 103   Place of Imprisonment 60

Rule 104   Supervision of Imprisonment 60

Rule 105   Restitution of Property 61

Rule 106   Compensation to Victims 62

Seven APPELLATE PROCEEDINGS 63

Rule 107   General Provision 63

Rule 108   Notice of Appeal 63

Rule 109   Record on Appeal 64

Rule 110   Copies of Record 64

Rule 111   Appellant's Brief 65

Rule 112   Respondent's Brief 65

Rule 113   Brief in Reply 65

Rule 114   Date of Hearing 65

Rule 115   Additional Evidence 66

Rule 116   Extension of Time-limits 66

Rule 116bis Expedited Appeals Procedure 66

Rule 117   Judgement on Appeal 67

Rule 118   Status of the Accused Following Appeal 67

Eight REVIEW PROCEEDINGS 68

Rule 119   Request for Review 68

Rule 120   Preliminary Examination 68

Rule 121   Appeals 68

Rule 122   Return of Case to Trial Chamber 69

Nine   PARDON AND COMMUTATION OF SENTENCE 70

Rule 123   Notification by States 70

Rule 124   Determination by the President 70

Rule 125   General Standards for Granting Pardon or
            Commutation 70

Part One

GENERAL PROVISIONS

Rule 1

Entry into Force

These Rules of Procedure and Evidence, adopted pursuant to Article 15 of the Statute of the Tribunal, shall come into force on 14 March 1994.

Rule 2

Definitions

(A) In the Rules, unless the context otherwise requires, the following terms shall mean:

Rules: The Rules referred to in Rule 1;

Statute: The Statute of the Tribunal adopted by Security Council resolution 827 of 25 May 1993;

Tribunal: The International Tribunal for the Prosecution of Persons Responsible for Serious Violations of International Humanitarian Law Committed in the Territory of the Former Yugoslavia since 1991, established by Security Council resolution 827 of 25 May 1993.

* * *

1

Accused:	A person against whom an indictment has been submitted in accordance with Rule 47;
Arrest:	The act of taking a suspect or an accused into custody by a national authority;
Bureau:	A body composed of the President, the Vice-President and the Presiding Judges of the Trial Chambers;
Investigation:	All activities undertaken by the Prosecutor under the Statute and the Rules for the collection of information and evidence;
Party:	The Prosecutor or the accused;
President:	The President of the Tribunal;
Prosecutor:	The Prosecutor appointed pursuant to Article 16 of the Statute;
Regulations:	The provisions framed by the Prosecutor pursuant to Sub-rule 37(A) for the purpose of directing the functions of his Office;
State:	A State Member or non-Member of the United Nations or a self-proclaimed entity de facto exercising governmental functions, whether recognised as a State or not;

Suspect:	A person concerning whom the Prosecutor possesses reliable information which tends to show that he may have committed a crime over which the Tribunal has jurisdiction;
Transaction:	A number of acts or omissions whether occurring as one event or a number of events, at the same or different locations and being part of a common scheme, strategy or plan;
Victim:	A person against whom a crime over which the Tribunal has jurisdiction has allegedly been committed.

(B)   In the Rules, the masculine shall include the feminine and the singular the plural, and vice-versa.

Rule 3
Languages

(A)   The working languages of the Tribunal shall be English and French.

(B)   An accused shall have the right to use his own language.

(C)   Any other person appearing before the Tribunal, other than as counsel, who does not have sufficient knowledge of either of the two working languages, may use his own language.

(D)   Counsel for an accused may apply to the Presiding Judge of a
        Chamber for leave to use a language other than the two
        working ones or the language of the accused. If such leave is
        granted, the expenses of interpretation and translation shall
        be borne by the Tribunal to the extent, if any, determined by
        the President, taking into account the rights of the defence
        and the interests of justice.

(E)   The Registrar shall make any necessary arrangements for
        interpretation and translation into and from the working
        languages.

Rule 4
Meetings away from the Seat of the Tribunal

A Chamber may exercise its functions at a place other than
the seat of the Tribunal, if so authorised by the President in the
interests of justice.

Rule 5
Non-compliance with Rules

Any objection by a party to an act of another party on the
ground of non-compliance with the Rules or Regulations shall be
raised at the earliest opportunity; it shall be upheld, and the act
declared null, only if the act was inconsistent with the
fundamental principles of fairness and has occasioned a miscarriage
of justice.

Rule 6

Amendment of the Rules

(A)   Proposals for amendment of the Rules may be made by a Judge, the Prosecutor or the Registrar and shall be adopted if agreed to by not less than seven Judges at a plenary meeting of the Tribunal convened with notice of the proposal addressed to all Judges.

(B)   An amendment to the Rules may be otherwise adopted, provided it is unanimously approved by the Judges.

(C)   An amendment shall enter into force immediately, but shall not operate to prejudice the rights of the accused in any pending case.

Rule 7

Authentic Texts

The English and French texts of the Rules shall be equally authentic. In case of discrepancy, the version which is more consonant with the spirit of the Statute and the Rules shall prevail.

Part Two

PRIMACY OF THE TRIBUNAL

Rule 8

Request for Information

Where it appears to the Prosecutor that a crime within the jurisdiction of the Tribunal is or has been the subject of investigations or criminal proceedings instituted in the courts of any State, he may request the State to forward to him all relevant information in that respect, and the State shall transmit to him such information forthwith in accordance with Article 29 of the Statute.

Rule 9

Prosecutor's Request for Deferral

Where it appears to the Prosecutor that in any such investigations or criminal proceedings instituted in the courts of any State:

(i)   the act being investigated or which is the subject of those proceedings is characterized as an ordinary crime;

(ii)   there is a lack of impartiality or independence, or the investigations or proceedings are designed to shield the accused from international criminal responsibility, or the case is not diligently prosecuted; or

(iii) what is in issue is closely related to, or otherwise involves, significant factual or legal questions which may have implications for investigations or prosecutions before the Tribunal,

the Prosecutor may propose to the Trial Chamber designated by the President that a formal request be made that such court defer to the competence of the Tribunal.

Rule 10
Formal Request for Deferral

(A) If it appears to the Trial Chamber seised of a proposal for deferral that, on any of the grounds specified in Rule 9, deferral is appropriate, the Trial Chamber may issue a formal request to the State concerned that its court defer to the competence of the Tribunal.

(B) A request for deferral shall include a request that the results of the investigation and a copy of the court's records and the judgement, if already delivered, be forwarded to the Tribunal.

(C) Where deferral to the Tribunal has been requested by a Trial Chamber, any subsequent trial shall be held before the other Trial Chamber.

Rule 11

Non-compliance with a Request for Deferral

If, within sixty days after a request for deferral has been notified by the Registrar to the State under whose jurisdiction the investigations or criminal proceedings have been instituted, the State fails to file a response which satisfies the Trial Chamber that the State has taken or is taking adequate steps to comply with the order, the Trial Chamber may request the President to report the matter to the Security Council.

Rule 12

Determinations of Courts of any State

Subject to Article 10(2) of the Statute, determinations of courts of any State are not binding on the Tribunal.

Rule 13

Non Bis in Idem

When the President receives reliable information to show that criminal proceedings have been instituted against a person before a court of any State for a crime for which that person has already been tried by the Tribunal, a Trial Chamber shall, following *mutatis mutandis* the procedure provided in Rule 10, issue a reasoned order requesting that court permanently to discontinue its proceedings. If that court fails to do so, the President may report the matter to the Security Council.

Part Three
ORGANIZATION OF THE TRIBUNAL

Section 1 The Judges

Rule 14
Solemn Declaration

(A) Before taking up his duties each Judge shall make the following solemn declaration:

"I solemnly declare that I will perform my duties and exercise my powers as a Judge of the International Tribunal for the Prosecution of Persons Responsible for Serious Violations of International Humanitarian Law Committed in the Territory of the Former Yugoslavia since 1991 honourably, faithfully, impartially and conscientiously".

(B) The declaration, signed by the Judge and witnessed by the Secretary-General of the United Nations or his representative, shall be kept in the records of the Tribunal.

Rule 15
Disqualification of Judges

(A) A Judge may not sit on a trial or appeal in any case in which he has a personal interest or concerning which he has or has had any association which might affect his impartiality. He shall in any such circumstance withdraw, and the President shall assign another Judge to sit in his place.

(B)   Any party may apply to the Presiding Judge of a Chamber for
        the disqualification and withdrawal of a Judge of that
        Chamber from a trial or appeal upon the above grounds. The
        Presiding Judge shall confer with the Judge in question, and
        if necessary the Bureau shall determine the matter. If the
        Bureau upholds the application, the President shall assign
        another Judge to sit in place of the disqualified Judge.

(C)   The Judge of the Trial Chamber who reviews an indictment
        against an accused, pursuant to Article 19 of the Statute and
        Rules 47 or 61, shall not sit as a member of the Trial
        Chamber for the trial of that accused.

(D)   No member of the Appeals Chamber shall sit on any appeal in a
        case in which he sat as a member of the Trial Chamber.

(E)   If a Judge is, for any reason, unable to continue sitting in
        a part-heard case, the Presiding Judge may, if that inability
        seems likely to be of short duration, adjourn the
        proceedings; otherwise he shall report to the President who
        may assign another Judge to the case and order either a
        rehearing or continuation of the proceedings from that point.
        However, after the opening statements provided for in Rule
        84, or the beginning of the presentation of evidence pursuant
        to Rule 85, the continuation of the proceedings can only be
        ordered with the consent of the accused.

Rule 16

Resignation

A Judge who decides to resign shall communicate his
resignation in writing to the President who shall transmit it to
the Secretary-General of the United Nations.

Rule 17

Precedence

(A) All Judges are equal in the exercise of their judicial functions, regardless of dates of election, appointment, age or period of service.

(B) The Presiding Judges of the Trial Chambers shall take precedence according to age after the President and the Vice-President.

(C) Judges elected or appointed on different dates shall take precedence according to the dates of their election or appointment; Judges elected or appointed on the same date shall take precedence according to age.

(D) In case of re-election, the total period of service as a Judge of the Tribunal shall be taken into account.

Section 2 The Presidency

Rule 18

Election of the President

(A) The President shall be elected for a term of two years, or such shorter term as shall coincide with the duration of his term of office as a Judge. He may be re-elected once.

(B) If the President ceases to be a member of the Tribunal or resigns his office before the expiration of his term, the Judges shall elect from among their number a successor for the remainder of the term.

(C) The President shall be elected by a majority of the votes of the Judges composing the Tribunal. If no Judge obtains such a majority, the second ballot shall be limited to the two Judges who obtained the greatest number of votes on the first ballot. In the case of equality of votes on the second ballot, the Judge who takes precedence in accordance with Rule 17 shall be declared elected.

Rule 19

Functions of the President

The President shall preside at all plenary meetings of the Tribunal; he shall coordinate the work of the Chambers and supervise the activities of the Registry as well as exercise all the other functions conferred on him by the Statute and the Rules.

Rule 20

The Vice-President

(A) The Vice-President shall be elected for a term of two years, or such shorter term as shall coincide with the duration of his term of office as a Judge. He may be re-elected once.

(B) The Vice-President may sit as a member of a Trial Chamber or of the Appeals Chamber.

(C) Sub-rules 18(B) and (C) shall apply *mutatis mutandis* to the Vice-President.

Rule 21

Functions of the Vice-President

Subject to Sub-rule 22(B), the Vice-President shall exercise the functions of the President in case of his absence or inability to act.

Rule 22

Replacements

(A)   If neither the President nor the Vice-President can carry out the functions of the President, these shall be assumed by the senior Judge, determined in accordance with Rule 17.

(B)   If the President is unable to exercise his functions as Presiding Judge of the Appeals Chamber, that Chamber shall elect a Presiding Judge from among its number.

Section 3 Internal Functioning of the Tribunal

Rule 23

The Bureau

(A)   The Bureau shall be composed of the President, the Vice-President and the Presiding Judges of the Trial Chambers.

(B)   The President shall consult the other members of the Bureau on all major questions relating to the functioning of the Tribunal.

(C)   A Judge may draw the attention of any member of the Bureau to issues that in his opinion ought to be discussed by the Bureau or submitted to a plenary meeting of the Tribunal.

Rule 24

Plenary Meetings of the Tribunal

The Judges shall meet in plenary to:

(i)   elect the President and Vice-President;

(ii)   adopt and amend the Rules;

(iii)   adopt the Annual Report provided for in Article 34 of the Statute;

(iv)   decide upon matters relating to the internal functioning of the Chambers and the Tribunal;

(v)   determine or supervise the conditions of detention;

(vi)   exercise any other functions provided for in the Statute or in the Rules.

Rule 25

Dates of Plenary Sessions

(A)   The dates of the plenary sessions of the Tribunal shall normally be agreed upon in July of each year for the following calendar year.

(B)   Other plenary meetings shall be convened by the President if so requested by at least six Judges, and may be convened whenever the exercise of his functions under the Statute or the Rules so requires.

Rule 26

Quorum and Vote

(A) The quorum for each plenary meeting of the Tribunal shall be seven Judges.

(B) Subject to Sub-rules 6(A) and (B) and Sub-rule 18(C), the decisions of the plenary meetings of the Tribunal shall be taken by the majority of the Judges present. In the event of an equality of votes, the President or the Judge who acts in his place shall have a casting vote.

Section 4 The Chambers

Rule 27

Rotation

(A) Judges shall rotate on a regular basis between the Trial Chambers and the Appeals Chamber. Rotation shall take into account the efficient disposal of cases.

(B) The Judges shall take their places in their new Chamber as soon as the President thinks it convenient, having regard to the disposal of part-heard cases.

(C) The President may at any time temporarily assign a member of a Trial Chamber or of the Appeals Chamber to another Chamber.

Rule 28

Assignment to Review Indictments

The President shall, in July of each year and after consultation with the Judges, assign for each month of the next calendar year one Judge from each Trial Chamber as the Judges to whom indictments shall be transmitted for review under Rule 47, and shall publish the list of assignments.

Rule 29

Deliberations

The deliberations of the Chambers shall take place in private and remain secret.

Section 5 The Registry

Rule 30

Appointment of the Registrar

The President shall seek the opinion of the Judges on the candidates for the post of Registrar, before consulting with the Secretary-General of the United Nations pursuant to Article 17(3) of the Statute.

Rule 31

Appointment of the Deputy Registrar and Registry Staff

The Registrar, after consultation with the Bureau, shall make his recommendations to the Secretary-General of the United Nations for the appointment of the Deputy Registrar and other Registry staff.

Rule 32

Solemn Declaration

(A)   Before taking up his duties, the Registrar shall make the following declaration before the President:

"I solemnly declare that I will perform the duties incumbent upon me as Registrar of the International Tribunal for the Prosecution of Persons Responsible for Serious Violations of International Humanitarian Law Committed in the Territory of the Former Yugoslavia since 1991 in all loyalty, discretion and good conscience and that I will faithfully observe all the provisions of the Statute and the Rules of Procedure and Evidence of the Tribunal".

(B)   Before taking up his duties, the Deputy Registrar shall make a similar declaration before the President.

(C)   Every staff member of the Registry shall make a similar declaration before the Registrar.

Rule 33

Functions of the Registrar

The Registrar shall assist the Chambers, the plenary meetings of the Tribunal, the Judges and the Prosecutor in the performance of their functions. Under the authority of the President, he shall be responsible for the administration and servicing of the Tribunal and shall serve as its channel of communication.

Rule 34

Victims and Witnesses Unit

(A)   There shall be set up under the authority of the Registrar a Victims and Witnesses Unit consisting of qualified staff to:

(i)   recommend protective measures for victims and witnesses in accordance with Article 22 of the Statute; and

(ii)   provide counselling and support for them, in particular in cases of rape and sexual assault.

(B)   Due consideration shall be given, in the appointment of staff, to the employment of qualified women.

Rule 35

Minutes

Except where a full record is made under Rule 81, the Registrar, or Registry staff designated by him, shall take minutes of the plenary meetings of the Tribunal and of the sittings of the Chambers, other than private deliberations.

Rule 36

Record Book

The Registrar shall keep a Record Book which shall list, subject to Rule 53, all the particulars of each case brought before the Tribunal. The Record Book shall be open to the public.

Section 6 The Prosecutor

Rule 37
Functions of the Prosecutor

(A) The Prosecutor shall perform all the functions provided by the Statute in accordance with the Rules and such Regulations, consistent with the Statute and the Rules, as may be framed by him. Any alleged inconsistency in the Regulations shall be brought to the attention of the Bureau to whose opinion the Prosecutor shall defer.

(B) His powers under Parts Four to Eight of the Rules may be exercised by staff members of the Office of the Prosecutor authorised by him, or by any person acting under his direction.

Rule 38
Deputy Prosecutor

(A) The Prosecutor shall make his recommendations to the Secretary-General of the United Nations for the appointment of a Deputy Prosecutor.

(B) The Deputy Prosecutor shall exercise the functions of the Prosecutor in the event of his absence or inability to act or upon the Prosecutor's express instructions.

Part Four

INVESTIGATIONS AND RIGHTS OF SUSPECTS

Section 1 Investigations

Rule 39

Conduct of Investigations

In the conduct of an investigation, the Prosecutor may:

(i)   summon and question suspects, victims and witnesses
        and record their statements, collect evidence and
        conduct on-site investigations;

(ii)   undertake such other matters as may appear necessary
        for completing the investigation and the preparation
        and conduct of the prosecution at the trial, including
        the taking of special measures to provide for the
        safety of potential witnesses and informants;

(iii)   seek, to that end, the assistance of any State
        authority concerned, as well as of any relevant
        international body including the International
        Criminal Police Organization (INTERPOL); and

(iv)   request such orders as may be necessary from a Trial
        Chamber or a Judge.

Rule 40

Provisional Measures

In case of urgency, the Prosecutor may request any State:

(i)   to arrest a suspect provisionally;

(ii)   to seize physical evidence;

(iii)   to take all necessary measures to prevent the escape of a suspect or an accused, injury to or intimidation of a victim or witness, or the destruction of evidence.

The State concerned shall comply forthwith, in accordance with Article 29 of the Statute.

Rule 41

Retention of Information

The Prosecutor shall be responsible for the retention, storage and security of information and physical evidence obtained in the course of his investigations.

Rule 42

Rights of Suspects during Investigation

(A)   A suspect who is to be questioned by the Prosecutor shall have the following rights, of which he shall be informed by the Prosecutor prior to questioning, in a language he speaks and understands:

(i)   the right to be assisted by counsel of his choice or
       to have legal assistance assigned to him without
       payment if he does not have sufficient means to pay
       for it;

(ii)   the right to have the free assistance of an
       interpreter if he cannot understand or speak the
       language to be used for questioning; and

(iii) the right to remain silent, and to be cautioned that
       any statement he makes shall be recorded and may be
       used in evidence.

(B)   Questioning of a suspect shall not proceed without the
       presence of counsel unless the suspect has voluntarily waived
       his right to counsel. In case of waiver, if the suspect
       subsequently expresses a desire to have counsel, questioning
       shall thereupon cease, and shall only resume when the suspect
       has obtained or has been assigned counsel.

Rule 43
Recording Questioning of Suspects

Whenever the Prosecutor questions a suspect, the questioning
shall be audio-recorded or video-recorded, in accordance with the
following procedure:

(i)   the suspect shall be informed in a language he speaks
       and understands that the questioning is being audio-
       recorded or video-recorded;

(ii)   in the event of a break in the course of the
       questioning, the fact and the time of the break shall
       be recorded before audio-recording or video-recording

ends and the time of resumption of the questioning shall also be recorded;

(iii)   at the conclusion of the questioning the suspect shall be offered the opportunity to clarify anything he has said, and to add anything he may wish, and the time of conclusion shall be recorded;

(iv)   the tape shall then be transcribed as soon as practicable after the conclusion of questioning and a copy of the transcript supplied to the suspect, together with a copy of the recorded tape or, if multiple recording apparatus was used, one of the original recorded tapes; and

(v)   after a copy has been made, if necessary, of the recorded tape for purposes of transcription, the original recorded tape or one of the original tapes shall be sealed in the presence of the suspect under the signature of the Prosecutor and the suspect.

Section 2 Of Counsel

Rule 44
Appointment and Qualifications of Counsel

Counsel engaged by a suspect or an accused shall file his power of attorney with the Registrar at the earliest opportunity. A counsel shall be considered qualified to represent a suspect or accused if he satisfies the Registrar that he is admitted to the practice of law in a State, or is a University professor of law.

Rule 45

Assignment of Counsel

(A)   A list of counsel who speak one or both of the working languages of the Tribunal, meet the requirements of Rule 44 and have indicated their willingness to be assigned by the Tribunal to indigent suspects or accused, shall be kept by the Registrar.

(B)   The criteria for determination of indigency shall be established by the Registrar and approved by the Judges.

(C)   In assigning counsel to an indigent suspect or accused, the following procedure shall be observed:

    (i)   a request for assignment of counsel shall be made to the Registrar;

    (ii)   the Registrar shall enquire into the means of the suspect or accused and determine whether the criteria of indigency are met;

    (iii) if he decides that the criteria are met, he shall assign counsel from the list; if he decides to the contrary, he shall inform the suspect or accused that the request is refused.

(D)   If a request is refused, a further request may be made by a suspect or an accused to the Registrar upon showing a change in circumstances.

(E)   The Registrar shall, in consultation with the Judges, establish the criteria for the payment of fees to assigned counsel.

(F)   If a suspect or an accused elects to conduct his own defence, he shall so notify the Registrar in writing at the first opportunity.

(G)   Where an alleged indigent person is subsequently found not to be indigent, the Chamber may make an order of contribution to recover the cost of providing counsel.

Rule 46
Misconduct of Counsel

(A)   A Chamber may, after a warning, refuse audience to counsel if, in its opinion, his conduct is offensive, abusive or otherwise obstructs the proper conduct of the proceedings.

(B)   A Judge or a Chamber may also, with the approval of the President, communicate any misconduct of counsel to the professional body regulating the conduct of counsel in his State of admission or, if a professor and not otherwise admitted to the profession, to the governing body of his University.

Part Five

PRE-TRIAL PROCEEDINGS

Section 1 Indictments

Rule 47

Submission of Indictment by the Prosecutor

(A)   If in the course of an investigation the Prosecutor is satisfied that there is sufficient evidence to provide reasonable grounds for believing that a suspect has committed a crime within the jurisdiction of the Tribunal, he shall prepare and forward to the Registrar an indictment for confirmation by a Judge, together with supporting material.

(B)   The indictment shall set forth the name and particulars of the suspect, and a concise statement of the facts of the case and of the crime with which the suspect is charged.

(C)   The Registrar shall forward the indictment and accompanying material to one of the Judges currently assigned under Rule 28, who will inform the Prosecutor of the date fixed for review of the indictment.

(D)   On reviewing the indictment, the Judge shall hear the Prosecutor, who may present additional material in support of any count. The Judge may confirm or dismiss each count or may adjourn the review.

(E)   The dismissal of a count in an indictment shall not preclude the Prosecutor from subsequently bringing a new indictment based on the acts underlying that count if supported by additional evidence.

Rule 48

Joinder of Accused

Persons accused of the same or different crimes committed in the course of the same transaction may be jointly charged and tried.

Rule 49

Joinder of Crimes

Two or more crimes may be joined in one indictment if the series of acts committed together form the same transaction, and the said crimes were committed by the same accused.

Rule 50

Amendment of Indictment

The Prosecutor may amend an indictment, without leave, at any time before its confirmation, but thereafter only with leave of the Judge who confirmed it or, ᵣif at trial, with leave of the Trial Chamber. If leave to amend is granted, the amended indictment shall be transmitted to the accused and to his counsel and where necessary the date for trial shall be postponed to ensure adequate time for the preparation of the defence.

Rule 51

Withdrawal of Indictment

(A)   The Prosecutor may withdraw an indictment, without leave, at any time before its confirmation, but thereafter only with leave of the Judge who confirmed it or, if at trial, only with leave of the Trial Chamber.

(B)   The withdrawal of the indictment shall be promptly notified
        to the suspect or the accused and to his counsel.

Rule 52
Public Character of Indictment

Subject to Rule 53, upon confirmation by a Judge of a Trial
Chamber, the indictment shall be made public.

Rule 53
Non-disclosure of Indictment

(A)   When confirming an indictment the Judge may, in consultation
        with the Prosecutor, order that there be no public disclosure
        of the indictment until it is served on the accused, or, in
        the case of joint accused, on all the accused.

(B)   A Judge or Trial Chamber may, in consultation with the
        Prosecutor, also order that there be no disclosure of an
        indictment, or part thereof, or of all or any part of any
        particular document or information, if satisfied that the
        making of such an order is required to give effect to a
        provision of the Rules, to protect confidential information
        obtained by the Prosecutor, or is otherwise in the interests
        of justice.

Section 2 Orders and Warrants

Rule 54

General Rule

At the request of either party or *proprio motu*, a Judge or a Trial Chamber may issue such orders, summonses, subpoenas, warrants and transfer orders as may be necessary for the purposes of an investigation or for the preparation or conduct of the trial.

Rule 55

Execution of Arrest Warrants

(A)   A warrant of arrest shall be signed by a Judge and shall bear the seal of the Tribunal. It shall be accompanied by a copy of the indictment, and a statement of the rights of the accused. These rights include those set forth in Article 21 of the Statute, and in Rules 42 and 43 *mutatis mutandis*, together with the right of the accused to remain silent, and to be cautioned that any statement he makes shall be recorded and may be used in evidence.

(B)   A warrant for the arrest of the accused and an order for his surrender to the Tribunal shall be transmitted by the Registrar to the national authorities of the State in whose territory or under whose jurisdiction or control the accused resides, or was last known to be, together with instructions that at the time of arrest the indictment and the statement of the rights of the accused be read to him in a language he understands and that he be cautioned in that language.

(C)   When an arrest warrant issued by the Tribunal is executed, a
       member of the Prosecutor's Office may be present as from the
       time of arrest.

Rule 56
Cooperation of States

The State to which a warrant of arrest or a transfer order
for a witness is transmitted shall act promptly and with all due
diligence to ensure proper and effective execution thereof, in
accordance with Article 29 of the Statute.

Rule 57
Procedure after Arrest

Upon the arrest of the accused, the State concerned shall
detain him, and shall promptly notify the Registrar. The transfer
of the accused to the seat of the Tribunal shall be arranged
between the State authorities concerned, the authorities of the
host country and the Registrar.

Rule 58
National Extradition Provisions

The obligations laid down in Article 29 of the Statute shall
prevail over any legal impediment to the surrender or transfer of
the accused or of a witness to the Tribunal which may exist under
the national law or extradition treaties of the State concerned.

Rule 59

Failure to Execute a Warrant or Transfer Order

(A)   Where the State to which a warrant of arrest or transfer order has been transmitted has been unable to execute the warrant, it shall report forthwith its inability to the Registrar, and the reasons therefor.

(B)   If, within a reasonable time after the warrant of arrest or transfer order has been transmitted to the State, no report is made on action taken, this shall be deemed a failure to execute the warrant of arrest or transfer order and the Tribunal, through the President, may notify the Security Council accordingly.

Rule 60

Advertisement of Indictment

At the request of the Prosecutor, a form of advertisement shall be transmitted by the Registrar to the national authorities of any State or States in whose territory the Prosecutor has reason to believe that the accused may be found, for publication in newspapers having wide circulation in that territory, intimating to the accused that service of an indictment against him is sought.

Rule 61

Procedure in Case of Failure to Execute a Warrant

(A)   If a warrant of arrest has not been executed, and personal service of the indictment has consequently not been effected, and the Prosecutor satisfies the Judge who confirmed the indictment that:

(i)   he has taken all reasonable steps to effect personal
        service, including recourse to the appropriate
        authorities of the State in whose territory or under
        whose jurisdiction and control the person to be served
        resides or was last known to him to be; and

(ii)   he has otherwise tried to inform the accused of the
        existence of the indictment by seeking publication of
        newspaper advertisements pursuant to Rule 60,

the Judge shall order that the indictment be submitted by the
Prosecutor to his Trial Chamber.

(B)   Upon obtaining such an order the Prosecutor shall submit the
        indictment to the Trial Chamber in open court, together with
        all the evidence that was before the Judge who initially
        confirmed the indictment. The Prosecutor may also call before
        the Trial Chamber and examine any witness whose statement has
        been submitted to the confirming Judge.

(C)   If the Trial Chamber is satisfied on that evidence, together
        with such additional evidence as the Prosecutor may tender,
        that there are reasonable grounds for believing that the
        accused has committed all or any of the crimes charged in the
        indictment, it shall so determine. The Trial Chamber shall
        have the relevant parts of the indictment read out by the
        Prosecutor together with an account of the efforts to effect
        service referred to in Sub-rule (A) above.

(D)   The Trial Chamber shall also issue an international arrest
        warrant in respect of the accused which shall be transmitted
        to all States.

(E)   If the Prosecutor satisfies the Trial Chamber that the failure to effect personal service was due in whole or in part to a failure or refusal of a State to cooperate with the Tribunal in accordance with Article 29 of the Statute, the Trial Chamber shall so certify, in which event the President shall notify the Security Council.

Rule 62

Initial Appearance of Accused

Upon his transfer to the seat of the Tribunal, the accused shall be brought before a Trial Chamber without delay, and shall be formally charged. The Trial Chamber shall:

(i)   satisfy itself that the right of the accused to counsel is respected;

(ii)   read or have the indictment read to the accused in a language he speaks and understands, and satisfy itself that the accused understands the indictment;

(iii) call upon the accused to enter a plea of guilty or not guilty on each count; should the accused fail to do so, enter a plea of not guilty on his behalf;

(iv)   in case of a plea of not guilty, instruct the Registrar to set a date for trial;

(v)   in case of a plea of guilty, instruct the Registrar to set a date for the pre-sentencing hearing;

(vi)   instruct the Registrar to set such other dates as appropriate.

Rule 63

Questioning of Accused

After the initial appearance of the accused the Prosecutor shall not question him unless his counsel is present and the questioning is tape-recorded or video-recorded in accordance with the procedure provided for in Rule 43. The Prosecutor shall at the beginning of the questioning caution the accused that he is not obliged to say anything unless he wishes to do so but that whatever he says may be given in evidence.

Rule 64

Detention on Remand

Upon his transfer to the seat of the Tribunal, the accused shall be detained in facilities provided by the host country, or by another country. The President may, on the application of a party, request modification of the conditions of detention of an accused.

Rule 65

Provisional Release

(A)   Once detained, an accused may not be released except upon an order of a Trial Chamber.

(B)   Release may be ordered by a Trial Chamber only in exceptional circumstances, after hearing the host country and only if it is satisfied that the accused will appear for trial and, if released, will not pose a danger to any victim, witness or other person.

(C)   The Trial Chamber may impose such conditions upon the release
        of the accused as it may determine appropriate, including the
        execution of a bail bond and the observance of such
        conditions as are necessary to ensure his presence for trial
        and the protection of others.

(D)   If necessary, the Trial Chamber may issue a warrant of arrest
        to secure the presence of an accused who has been released or
        is for any other reason at liberty.

Section 3 Production of Evidence

Rule 66
Disclosure by the Prosecutor

(A)   The Prosecutor shall make available to the defence, as soon
        as practicable after the initial appearance of the accused,
        copies of the supporting material which accompanied the
        indictment when confirmation was sought as well as all prior
        statements obtained by the Prosecutor from the accused or
        from prosecution witnesses.

(B)   The Prosecutor shall on request, subject to Sub-rule (C),
        permit the defence to inspect any books, documents,
        photographs and tangible objects in his custody or control,
        which are material to the preparation of the defence, or are
        intended for use by the Prosecutor as evidence at trial or
        were obtained from or belonged to the accused.

(C)   Where information is in the possession of the Prosecutor, the
        disclosure of which may prejudice further or ongoing
        investigations, or for any other reasons may be contrary to
        the public interest or affect the security interests of any
        State, the Prosecutor may apply to the Trial Chamber sitting
        in camera to be relieved from the obligation to disclose
        pursuant to Sub-rule (B). When making such application the
        Prosecutor shall provide the Trial Chamber (but only the
        Trial Chamber) with the information that is sought to be kept
        confidential.

Rule 67

Reciprocal Disclosure

(A)   As early as reasonably practicable and in any event prior to
        the commencement of the trial:

   (i)   the Prosecutor shall notify the defence of the names
          of the witnesses that he intends to call in proof of
          the guilt of the accused and in rebuttal of any
          defence plea of which the Prosecutor has received
          notice in accordance with Sub-rule (ii) below;

   (ii)   the defence shall notify the Prosecutor of its intent
          to offer:

      (a)   the defence of alibi; in which case the
             notification shall specify the place or places
             at which the accused claims to have been
             present at the time of the alleged crime and
             the names and addresses of witnesses and any
             other evidence upon which the accused intends
             to rely to establish the alibi;

(b)   any special defence, including that of diminished or lack of mental responsibility; in which case the notification shall specify the names and addresses of witnesses and any other evidence upon which the accused intends to rely to establish the special defence.

(B)   Failure of the defence to provide notice under this Rule shall not limit the right of the accused to testify on the above defences.

(C)   If the defence makes a request pursuant to Sub-rule 66(B), the Prosecutor shall be entitled to inspect any books, documents, photographs and tangible objects, which are within the custody or control of the defence and which it intends to use as evidence at the trial.

(D)   If either party discovers additional evidence or material which should have been produced earlier pursuant to the Rules, that party shall promptly notify the other party and the Trial Chamber of the existence of the additional evidence or material.

Rule 68
Disclosure of Exculpatory Evidence

The Prosecutor shall, as soon as practicable, disclose to the defence the existence of evidence known to the Prosecutor which in any way tends to suggest the innocence or mitigate the guilt of the accused or may affect the credibility of prosecution evidence.

Rule 69
Protection of Victims and Witnesses

(A)   In exceptional circumstances, the Prosecutor may apply to a Trial Chamber to order the non-disclosure of the identity of a victim or witness who may be in danger or at risk until such person is brought under the protection of the Tribunal.

(B)   In the determination of protective measures for victims and witnesses, the Trial Chamber may consult the Victims and Witnesses Unit.

(C)   Subject to Rule 75, the identity of the victim or witness shall be disclosed in sufficient time prior to the trial to allow adequate time for preparation of the defence.

Rule 70
Matters not Subject to Disclosure

(A)   Notwithstanding the provisions of Rules 66 and 67, reports, memoranda, or other internal documents prepared by a party, its assistants or representatives in connection with the investigation or preparation of the case, are not subject to disclosure or notification under those Rules.

(B)   If the Prosecutor is in possession of information which has been provided to him on a confidential basis and which has been used solely for the purpose of generating new evidence, that initial information and its origin shall not be disclosed by the Prosecutor without the consent of the person or entity providing the initial information and shall in any event not be given in evidence without prior disclosure to the accused.

(C)   If, after obtaining the consent of the person or entity providing information under this Rule, the Prosecutor elects to present as evidence any testimony, document or other material so provided, the Trial Chamber, notwithstanding Rule 98, may not order either party to produce additional evidence received from the person or entity providing the initial information, nor may the Trial Chamber for the purpose of obtaining such additional evidence itself summon that person or a representative of that entity as a witness or order their attendance.

(D)   If the Prosecutor calls as a witness the person providing, or a representative of the entity providing, information under this Rule, the Trial Chamber may not compel the witness to answer any question the witness declines to answer on grounds of confidentiality.

(E)   The right of the accused to challenge the evidence presented by the Prosecution shall remain unaffected subject only to limitations contained in Sub-rules (C) and (D).

(F)   Nothing in Sub-rule (C) or (D) above shall effect a Trial Chamber's power under Rule 89(D) to exclude evidence if its probative value is substantially outweighed by the need to ensure a fair trial.

Section 4 Depositions

Rule 71
Depositions

(A) At the request of either party, a Trial Chamber may, in exceptional circumstances and in the interests of justice, order that a deposition be taken for use at trial, and appoint, for that purpose, a Presiding Officer.

(B) The motion for the taking of a deposition shall be in writing and shall indicate the name and whereabouts of the person whose deposition is sought, the date and place at which the deposition is to be taken, a statement of the matters on which the person is to be examined, and of the exceptional circumstances justifying the taking of the deposition.

(C) If the motion is granted, the party at whose request the deposition is to be taken shall give reasonable notice to the other party, who shall have the right to attend the taking of the deposition and cross-examine the person whose deposition is being taken.

(D) Deposition evidence may also be given by means of a video-conference.

(E) The Presiding Officer shall ensure that the deposition is taken in accordance with the Rules and that a record is made of the deposition, including cross-examination and objections raised by either party for decision by the Trial Chamber. He shall transmit the record to the Trial Chamber.

Section 5 Preliminary Motions

Rule 72
General Provisions

(A) After the initial appearance of the accused, either party may move before a Trial Chamber for appropriate relief or ruling. Such motions may be written or oral, at the discretion of the Trial Chamber.

(B) The Trial Chamber shall dispose of preliminary motions *in limine litis* and without interlocutory appeal, save in the case of dismissal of an objection based on lack of jurisdiction.

Rule 73
Preliminary Motions by Accused

(A) Preliminary motions by the accused shall include:

(i) objections based on lack of jurisdiction;

(ii) objections based on defects in the form of the indictment;

(iii) applications for the exclusion of evidence obtained from the accused or having belonged to him;

(iv) applications for severance of crimes joined in one indictment under Rule 49, or for separate trials under Sub-rule 82(B);

(v) objections based on the denial of request for assignment of counsel.

(B)   Any of the motions by the accused referred to in Sub-rule (A) shall be brought within sixty days after his initial appearance, and in any case before the hearing on the merits.

(C)   Failure to apply within the time-limit prescribed shall constitute a waiver of the right. Upon a showing of good cause, the Trial Chamber may grant relief from the waiver.

Part Six

PROCEEDINGS BEFORE TRIAL CHAMBERS

Section 1 General Provisions

Rule 74

Amicus Curiae

A Chamber may, if it considers it desirable for the proper determination of the case, invite or grant leave to a State, organization or person to appear before it and make submissions on any issue specified by the Chamber.

Rule 75

Measures for the Protection of Victims and Witnesses

(A)   A Judge or a Chamber may, *proprio motu* or at the request of either party, or of the victim or witness concerned, or of the Victims and Witnesses Unit, order appropriate measures for the privacy and protection of victims and witnesses, provided that the measures are consistent with the rights of the accused.

(B)   A Chamber may hold an *in camera* proceeding to determine whether to order:

    (i)   measures to prevent disclosure to the public or the media of the identity or whereabouts of a victim or a witness, or of persons related to or associated with him by such means as:

(a)   expunging names and identifying information
        from the Chamber's public records;

(b)   non-disclosure to the public of any records
        identifying the victim;

(c)   giving of testimony through image- or voice-
        altering devices or closed circuit television;
        and

(d)   assignment of a pseudonym;

(ii)   closed sessions, in accordance with Rule 79;

(iii)   appropriate measures to facilitate the testimony of
        vulnerable victims and witnesses, such as one-way
        closed circuit television.

(C)   A Chamber shall, whenever necessary, control the manner of
        questioning to avoid any harassment or intimidation.

Rule 76
Solemn Declaration by Interpreters and Translators

Before performing any duties, an interpreter or a translator
shall solemnly declare to do so faithfully, independently,
impartially and with full respect for the duty of confidentiality.

Rule 77

Contempt of the Tribunal

(A) Subject to the provisions of Sub-rule 90(E), a witness who refuses or fails contumaciously to answer a question relevant to the issue before a Chamber may be found in contempt of the Tribunal. The Chamber may impose a fine not exceeding US$10,000 or a term of imprisonment not exceeding six months.

(B) The Chamber may, however, relieve the witness of the duty to answer, for reasons which it deems appropriate.

(C) Any person who attempts to interfere with or intimidate a witness may be found guilty of contempt and sentenced in accordance with Sub-rule (A).

(D) Any judgement rendered under this Rule shall be subject to appeal.

(E) Payment of a fine shall be made to the Registrar to be held in a separate account.

Rule 78

Open Sessions

All proceedings before a Trial Chamber, other than deliberations of the Chamber, shall be held in public, unless otherwise provided.

Rule 79
Closed Sessions

(A)   The Trial Chamber may order that the press and the public be excluded from all or part of the proceedings for reasons of:

(i)   public order or morality;

(ii)   safety, security or non-disclosure of the identity of a victim or witness as provided in Rule 75; or

(iii) the protection of the interests of justice.

(B)   The Trial Chamber shall make public the reasons for its order.

Rule 80
Control of Proceedings

(A)   The Trial Chamber may exclude a person from the courtroom in order to protect the right of the accused to a fair and public trial, or to maintain the dignity and decorum of the proceedings.

(B)   The Trial Chamber may order the removal of an accused from the courtroom and continue the proceedings in his absence if he has persisted in disruptive conduct following a warning that he may be removed.

46

Rule 81

Records of Proceedings and Evidence

(A)   The Registrar shall cause to be made and preserve a full and accurate record of all proceedings, including audio recordings, transcripts and, when deemed necessary by the Trial Chamber, video recordings.

(B)   The Trial Chamber may order the disclosure of all or part of the record of closed proceedings when the reasons for ordering its non-disclosure no longer exist.

(C)   The Registrar shall retain and preserve all physical evidence offered during the proceedings.

(D)   Photography, video-recording or audio-recording of the trial, otherwise than by the Registry, may be authorised at the discretion of the Trial Chamber.

Section 2 Case Presentation

Rule 82

Joint and Separate Trials

(A)   In joint trials, each accused shall be accorded the same rights as if he were being tried separately.

(B)   The Trial Chamber may order that persons accused jointly under Rule 48 be tried separately if it considers it necessary in order to avoid a conflict of interests that might cause serious prejudice to an accused, or to protect the interests of justice.

Rule 83

Instruments of Restraint

Instruments of restraint, such as handcuffs, shall not be used except as a precaution against escape during transfer or for security reasons, and shall be removed when the accused appears before a Chamber.

Rule 84

Opening Statements

Before presentation of evidence by the Prosecutor, each party may make an opening statement. The defence may however elect to make its statement after the Prosecutor has concluded his presentation of evidence and before the presentation of evidence for the defence.

Rule 85

Presentation of Evidence

(A)   Each party is entitled to call witnesses and present evidence. Unless otherwise directed by the Trial Chamber in the interests of justice, evidence at the trial shall be presented in the following sequence:

(i)   evidence for the prosecution;

(ii)   evidence for the defence;

(iii) prosecution evidence in rebuttal;

(iv)   defence evidence in rejoinder;

(v)   evidence ordered by the Trial Chamber pursuant to
        Rule 98.

(B)   Examination-in-chief, cross-examination and re-examination
        shall be allowed in each case. It shall be for the party
        calling a witness to examine him in chief, but a Judge may at
        any stage put any question to the witness.

(C)   The accused may, if he so desires, appear as a witness in his
        own defence.

Rule 86

Closing Arguments

After the presentation of all the evidence, the Prosecutor
may present an initial argument, to which the defence may reply.
The Prosecutor may, if he wishes, present a rebuttal argument, to
which the defence may present a rejoinder.

Rule 87

Deliberations

(A)   When both parties have completed their presentation of the
        case, the Presiding Judge shall declare the hearing closed,
        and the Trial Chamber shall deliberate in private. A finding
        of guilt may be reached only when a majority of the Trial
        Chamber is satisfied that guilt has been proved beyond
        reasonable doubt.

(B)   The Trial Chamber shall vote separately on each charge
        contained in the indictment. If two or more accused are tried
        together under Rule 48, separate findings shall be made as to
        each accused.

Rule 88

Judgement

(A)   The judgement shall be pronounced in public, on a date of
        which notice shall have been given to the parties and counsel
        and at which they shall be entitled to be present.

(B)   If the Trial Chamber finds the accused guilty of a crime and
        concludes from the evidence that unlawful taking of property
        by the accused was associated with it, it shall make a
        specific finding to that effect in its judgement. The Trial
        Chamber may order restitution as provided in Rule 105.

(C)   The judgement shall be rendered by a majority of the Judges.
        It shall be accompanied or followed as soon as possible by a
        reasoned opinion in writing, to which separate or dissenting
        opinions may be appended.

Section 3 Rules of Evidence

Rule 89
General Provisions

(A)   The rules of evidence set forth in this Section shall govern the proceedings before the Chambers. The Chambers shall not be bound by national rules of evidence.

(B)   In cases not otherwise provided for in this Section, a Chamber shall apply rules of evidence which will best favour a fair determination of the matter before it and are consonant with the spirit of the Statute and the general principles of law.

(C)   A Chamber may admit any relevant evidence which it deems to have probative value.

(D)   A Chamber may exclude evidence if its probative value is substantially outweighed by the need to ensure a fair trial.

(E)   A Chamber may request verification of the authenticity of evidence obtained out of court.

Rule 90

Testimony of Witnesses

(A)   Witnesses shall, in principle, be heard directly by the Chambers unless a Chamber has ordered that the witness be heard by means of a deposition as provided for in Rule 71.

(B)   Every witness shall, before giving evidence, make the following solemn declaration: "I solemnly declare that I will speak the truth, the whole truth and nothing but the truth".

(C)   A child who, in the opinion of the Chamber, does not understand the nature of a solemn declaration, may be permitted to testify without that formality, if the Chamber is of the opinion that he is sufficiently mature to be able to report the facts of which he had knowledge and that he understands the duty to tell the truth. A judgement, however, cannot be based on such testimony alone.

(D)   A witness, other than an expert, who has not yet testified shall not be present when the testimony of another witness is given. However, a witness who has heard the testimony of another witness shall not for that reason alone be disqualified from testifying.

(E)   A witness may object to making any statement which might tend to incriminate him. The Chamber may, however, compel the witness to answer the question. Testimony compelled in this way shall not be used as evidence in a subsequent prosecution against the witness for any offence other than perjury.

Rule 90 *bis*

Transfer of a Detained Witness

(A)   Any detained person whose personal appearance as a witness has been requested by the Tribunal shall be transferred temporarily to the detention unit of the Tribunal, conditional on his return within the period decided by the Tribunal.

(B)   The transfer order shall be issued by a Judge or Trial Chamber only after prior verification that the following conditions have been met:

    (i)   the presence of the detained witness is not required for any criminal proceedings in progress in the territory of the requested State during the period the witness is required by the Tribunal;

    (ii)   transfer of the witness does not extend the period of his detention as foreseen by the requested State;

(C)   The Registry shall transmit the order of transfer to the national authorities of the State on whose territory, or under whose jurisdiction or control, the witness is detained. Transfer shall be arranged by the national authorities concerned in liaison with the host country and the Registrar.

(D)   The Registry shall ensure the proper conduct of the transfer, including the supervision of the witness in the detention unit of the Tribunal; it shall remain abreast of any changes which might occur regarding the conditions of detention provided for by the requested State and which may possibly affect the length of the detention of the witness in the detention unit and, as promptly as possible, shall inform the relevant Judge or Chamber.

(E)   On expiration of the period decided by the Tribunal for the temporary transfer, the detained witness shall be remanded to the authorities of the requested State, unless the State, within that period, has transmitted an order of release of the witness, which shall take effect immediately.

(F)   If, by the end of the period decided by the Tribunal, the presence of the detained witness continues to be necessary, a Judge or Chamber may extend the period on the same conditions as stated in Sub-rule (B).

Rule 91
False Testimony under Solemn Declaration

(A)   A Chamber, on its own initiative or at the request of a party, may warn a witness of the duty to tell the truth and the consequences that may result from a failure to do so.

(B)   If a Chamber has strong grounds for believing that a witness has knowingly and wilfully given false testimony, it may direct the Prosecutor to investigate the matter with a view to the preparation and submission of an indictment for false testimony.

(C)   The rules of procedure and evidence in Parts Four to Eight shall apply *mutatis mutandis* to proceedings under this Rule.

(D)   No Judge who sat as a member of the Trial Chamber before which the witness appeared shall sit for the trial of the witness for false testimony.

(E) The maximum penalty for false testimony under solemn declaration shall be a fine of US$10,000 or a term of imprisonment of twelve months, or both. The payment of any fine imposed shall be made to the Registrar to be held in the account referred to in Sub-rule 77(E).

Rule 92

Confessions

A confession by the accused given during questioning by the Prosecutor shall, provided the requirements of Rule 63 were strictly complied with, be presumed to have been free and voluntary unless the contrary is proved.

Rule 93

Evidence of Consistent Pattern of Conduct

(A) Evidence of a consistent pattern of conduct relevant to serious violations of international humanitarian law under the Statute may be admissible in the interests of justice.

(B) Acts tending to show such a pattern of conduct shall be disclosed by the Prosecutor to the defence pursuant to Rule 66.

Rule 94

Judicial Notice

A Trial Chamber shall not require proof of facts of common knowledge but shall take judicial notice thereof.

Rule 95

Evidence Obtained by Means Contrary to Internationally Protected Human Rights

No evidence shall be admissible if obtained by methods which cast substantial doubt on its reliability or if its admission is antithetical to, and would seriously damage, the integrity of the proceedings.

Rule 96

Evidence in Cases of Sexual Assault

In cases of sexual assault:

(i)   no corroboration of the victim's testimony shall be required;

(ii)   consent shall not be allowed as a defence if the victim

    (a)   has been subjected to or threatened with or has had reason to fear violence, duress, detention or psychological oppression, or

    (b)   reasonably believed that if the victim did not submit, another might be so subjected, threatened or put in fear;

(iii)   before evidence of the victim's consent is admitted, the accused shall satisfy the Trial Chamber *in camera* that the evidence is relevant and credible;

(iv)   prior sexual conduct of the victim shall not be admitted in evidence.

Rule 97

Lawyer-Client Privilege

All communications between lawyer and client shall be regarded as privileged, and consequently not subject to disclosure at trial, unless:

(i)   the client consents to such disclosure; or

(ii)   the client has voluntarily disclosed the content of the communication to a third party, and that third party then gives evidence of that disclosure.

Rule 98

Power of Chambers to Order Production of Additional Evidence

A Trial Chamber may order either party to produce additional evidence. It may itself summon witnesses and order their attendance.

Section 4 Sentencing Procedure

Rule 99

Status of the Acquitted Person

(A)   In case of acquittal, the accused shall be released
      immediately.

(B)   If, at the time the judgement is pronounced, the Prosecutor
      advises the Trial Chamber in open court of his intention to
      file notice of appeal pursuant to Rule 108, the Trial Chamber
      may, at the request of the Prosecutor, issue a warrant for
      the arrest of the accused to take effect immediately.

Rule 100

Pre-sentencing Procedure

If a Trial Chamber finds the accused guilty of a crime, the
Prosecutor and the defence may submit any relevant information that
may assist the Trial Chamber in determining an appropriate
sentence.

Rule 101

Penalties

(A)   A convicted person may be sentenced to imprisonment for a
      term up to and including the remainder of his life.

(B)   In determining the sentence, the Trial Chamber shall take
        into account the factors mentioned in Article 24(2) of the
        Statute, as well as such factors as:

        (i)   any aggravating circumstances;

        (ii)   any mitigating circumstances including the substantial
                cooperation with the Prosecutor by the convicted
                person before or after conviction;

        (iii)   the general practice regarding prison sentences in the
                courts of the former Yugoslavia;

        (iv)   the extent to which any penalty imposed by a court of
                any State on the convicted person for the same act has
                already been served, as referred to in Article 10(3)
                of the Statute.

(C)   The Trial Chamber shall indicate whether multiple sentences
        shall be served consecutively or concurrently.

(D)   The sentence shall be pronounced in public and in the
        presence of the convicted person, subject to Sub-rule 102(B).

(E)   Credit shall be given to the convicted person for the period,
        if any, during which the convicted person was detained in
        custody pending his surrender to the Tribunal or pending
        trial or appeal.

Rule 102

Status of the Convicted Person

(A)   The sentence shall begin to run from the day it is pronounced under Sub-rule 101(D). However, as soon as notice of appeal is given, the enforcement of the judgement shall thereupon be stayed until the decision on the appeal has been delivered, the convicted person meanwhile remaining in detention, as provided in Rule 64.

(B)   If, by a previous decision of the Trial Chamber, the convicted person has been released, or is for any other reason at liberty, and he is not present when the judgement is pronounced, the Trial Chamber shall issue a warrant for his arrest. On arrest, he shall be notified of the conviction and sentence, and the procedure provided in Rule 103 shall be followed.

Rule 103

Place of Imprisonment

(A)   Imprisonment shall be served in a State designated by the Tribunal from a list of States which have indicated their willingness to accept convicted persons.

(B)   Transfer of the convicted person to that State shall be effected as soon as possible after the time-limit for appeal has elapsed.

Rule 104

Supervision of Imprisonment

All sentences of imprisonment shall be supervised by the Tribunal or a body designated by it.

Rule 105

Restitution of Property

(A) After a judgement of conviction containing a specific finding as provided in Sub-rule 88(B), the Trial Chamber shall, at the request of the Prosecutor, or may, at its own initiative, hold a special hearing to determine the matter of the restitution of the property or the proceeds thereof, and may in the meantime order such provisional measures for the preservation and protection of the property or proceeds as it considers appropriate.

(B) The determination may extend to such property or its proceeds, even in the hands of third parties not otherwise connected with the crime of which the convicted person has been found guilty.

(C) Such third parties shall be summoned before the Trial Chamber and be given an opportunity to justify their claim to the property or its proceeds.

(D) Should the Trial Chamber be able to determine the rightful owner on the balance of probabilities, it shall order the restitution either of the property or the proceeds or make such other order as it may deem appropriate.

(E) Should the Trial Chamber not be able to determine ownership, it shall notify the competent national authorities and request them so to determine.

(F) Upon notice from the national authorities that an affirmative determination has been made, the Trial Chamber shall order the restitution either of the property or the proceeds or make such other order as it may deem appropriate.

(G)   The Registrar shall transmit to the competent national
        authorities any summonses, orders and requests issued by a
        Trial Chamber pursuant to Sub-rules (C),(D),(E) and (F).

Rule 106
Compensation to Victims

(A)   The Registrar shall transmit to the competent authorities of
        the States concerned the judgement finding the accused guilty
        of a crime which has caused injury to a victim.

(B)   Pursuant to the relevant national legislation, a victim or
        persons claiming through him may bring an action in a
        national court or other competent body to obtain
        compensation.

(C)   For the purposes of a claim made under Sub-rule (B) the
        judgement of the Tribunal shall be final and binding as to
        the criminal responsibility of the convicted person for such
        injury.

Part Seven
APPELLATE PROCEEDINGS

Rule 107
General Provision

The rules of procedure and evidence that govern proceedings in the Trial Chambers shall apply *mutatis mutandis* to proceedings in the Appeals Chamber.

Rule 108
Notice of Appeal

(A)   Subject to Sub-rule (B), a party seeking to appeal a judgement or sentence shall, not more than thirty days from the date on which the judgement or sentence was pronounced, file with the Registrar and serve upon the other parties a written notice of appeal, setting forth the grounds.

(B)   Such delay shall be fixed at fifteen days in case of an appeal from a judgement dismissing an objection based on lack of jurisdiction or a decision rendered under Rule 77 or Rule 91.

Rule 109
Record on Appeal

(A)   The record on appeal shall consist of the parts of the trial record, as certified by the Registrar, designated by the parties.

(B)   The parties, within thirty days of the certification of the trial record by the Registrar, may by agreement designate the parts of that record which, in their opinion, are necessary for the decision on the appeal.

(C)   Should the parties fail so to agree within that time, the Appellant and the Respondent shall each designate to the Registrar, within sixty days of the certification, the parts of the trial record which he considers necessary for the decision on the appeal.

(D)   The Appeals Chamber shall remain free to call for the whole of the trial record.

Rule 110
Copies of Record

The Registrar shall make a sufficient number of copies of the record on appeal for the use of the Judges of the Appeals Chamber and of the parties.

Rule 111

Appellant's Brief

An Appellant's brief of argument and authorities shall be served on the other party and filed with the Registrar within ninety days of the certification of the record.

Rule 112

Respondent's Brief

A Respondent's brief of argument and authorities shall be served on the other party and filed with the Registrar within thirty days of the filing of the Appellant's brief.

Rule 113

Brief in Reply

An Appellant may file a brief in reply within fifteen days after the filing of the Respondent's brief.

Rule 114

Date of Hearing

After the expiry of the time-limits for filing the briefs provided for in Rules 111, 112 and 113, the Appeals Chamber shall set the date for the hearing and the Registrar shall notify the parties.

Rule 115

Additional Evidence

(A)   A party may apply by motion to present before the Appeals Chamber additional evidence which was not available to it at the trial. Such motion must be served on the other party and filed with the Registrar not less than fifteen days before the date of the hearing.

(B)   The Appeals Chamber shall authorise the presentation of such evidence if it considers that the interests of justice so require.

Rule 116

Extension of Time-limits

The Appeals Chamber may grant a motion to extend a time-limit upon a showing of good cause.

Rule 116 *bis*

Expedited Appeals Procedure

(A)   An appeal under Sub-rule 108(B) shall be heard expeditiously on the basis of the original record of the Trial Chamber and without the necessity of any written brief.

(B)   All delays and other procedural requirements shall be fixed by an order of the President issued on an application by one of the parties, or *proprio moto* should no such application have been made within fifteen days after the filing of the notice of appeal.

(C)   Rules 109 to 114 shall not apply to such appeals.

Rule 117

Judgement on Appeal

(A)   The Appeals Chamber shall pronounce judgement on the basis of the record on appeal together with such additional evidence as has been presented to it.

(B)   The judgement shall be rendered by a majority of the Judges. It shall be accompanied or followed as soon as possible by a reasoned opinion in writing, to which separate or dissenting opinions may be appended.

(C)   In appropriate circumstances the Appeals Chamber may order that the accused be retried according to law.

(D)   The judgement shall be pronounced in public, on a date of which notice shall have been given to the parties and counsel and at which they shall be entitled to be present.

Rule 118

Status of the Accused Following Appeal

(A)   A sentence pronounced by the Appeals Chamber shall be enforced immediately.

(B)   Where the accused is not present when the judgement is due to be delivered, either as having been acquitted on all charges or as a result of an order issued pursuant to Rule 65, or for any other reason, the Appeals Chamber may deliver its judgement in the absence of the accused and shall, unless it pronounces his acquittal, order his arrest or surrender to the Tribunal.

Part Eight
REVIEW PROCEEDINGS

Rule 119
Request for Review

Where a new fact has been discovered which was not known to the moving party at the time of the proceedings before a Trial Chamber or the Appeals Chamber, and could not have been discovered through the exercise of due diligence, the defence or, within one year after the final judgement has been pronounced, the Prosecutor, may make a motion to that Chamber for review of the judgement.

Rule 120
Preliminary Examination

If a majority of Judges of the Chamber that pronounced the judgement agree that the new fact, if proved, could have been a decisive factor in reaching a decision, the Chamber shall review the judgement, and pronounce a further judgement after hearing the parties.

Rule 121
Appeals

The judgement of a Trial Chamber on review may be appealed in accordance with the provisions of Part Seven.

Rule 122

Return of Case to Trial Chamber

If the judgement to be reviewed is under appeal at the time the motion for review is filed, the Appeals Chamber may return the case to the Trial Chamber for disposition of the motion.

Part Nine

PARDON AND COMMUTATION OF SENTENCE

Rule 123

Notification by States

If, according to the law of the State in which a convicted person is imprisoned, he is eligible for pardon or commutation of sentence, the State shall, in accordance with Article 28 of the Statute, notify the Tribunal of such eligibility.

Rule 124

Determination by the President

The President shall, upon such notice, determine, in consultation with the Judges, whether pardon or commutation is appropriate.

Rule 125

General Standards for Granting Pardon or Commutation

In determining whether pardon or commutation is appropriate, the President shall take into account, *inter alia*, the gravity of the crime or crimes for which the prisoner was convicted, the treatment of similarly-situated prisoners, the prisoner's demonstration of rehabilitation, as well as any substantial cooperation of the prisoner with the Prosecutor.

ORGANISATION OF THE TRIBUNAL

PRESIDING JUDGE OF THE TRIBUNAL:
- presides over all the plenary session the Tribunal
- coordinates the work of the courts
- supervises the work of the Registrar

DEPUTY PRESIDING JUDGE
- performs the functions of the Presiding Judge if the latter is absent or otherwise prevented from attending court

PLENARY SESSIONS

- composition = panel of 11 judges
- quorum = 7 judges
- vote = taken by the majority of judges present

ROLE

- Election of the Presiding judge and Deputy Presiding judge
- Adoption and modification of the Rules
- Adoption of decisions on issues relating to the internal operation of the Tribunal
- Determination or control of the conditions of detention

BUREAU

- Presiding judge
- Deputy Presiding judge
- the two Presiding judges of the lower court

Examination of all the important issues relating to the operation of the tribunal

STRUCTURE OF THE COURT

COURT OF THE FIRST INSTANCE

Presiding judge elected by the panel of judges

2 judges

COURT OF THE FIRST INSTANCE

Presiding judge elected by the panel of judges

2 judges

Conduct of proceeding in the court over which he/she presides

COURT OF APPEAL

Presiding judge = President of the court

if the presiding judge is absent or the panel of judges is prevented from electing a presiding judge

Conduct of the proceedings

4 judges

OFFICE OF THE REGISTRAR

- administration and services of the court
- organisation shared by the courts and the Prosecutor

REGISTRAR

Appointed by the Secretary-General after consultation with the Presiding judge for a four-year renewable term of office.
> responsible for the courts administration
> responsible for all correspondence from and to the courts

REGISTER OFFICE

Appointed by the Secretary-General on the recommendation of the Registrar.
> assists the Registrar

| Assistant Registrar | Other staff |

Victim and Witness Assistance Department

- recommends application of Protection Orders
- advice and assistance

INVESTIGATION AND PROSECUTION

- investigation of cases
- creation of prosecution case
- initiation of prosecution

PROSECUTOR

Appointed by the Security Council on the recommendation of the Secretary General for a four-year renewable term of office.
> responsible for investigating cases and prosecuting them

OFFICE OF THE PROSECUTOR

Appointed by the Secretary General at the recommendation of the Prosecutor
> Deputy Prosecutor: fulfills the office of the Prosecutor in the latter's absence, illness or on the latter's official instruction.
> other staff

| Investigation Section | Prosecution Section |

OPERATION OF THE TRIBUNAL

GOVERNMENTS INTERGOVERNMENTAL ORGANISATIONS NGOs UN ORGANISATIONS VICTIMS

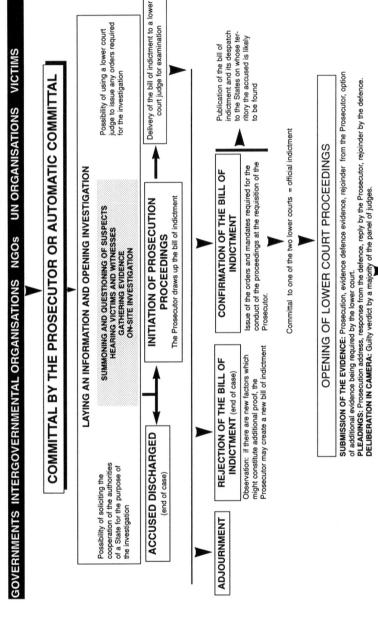

COMMITTAL BY THE PROSECUTOR OR AUTOMATIC COMMITTAL

LAYING AN INFORMATION AND OPENING INVESTIGATION

Possibility of soliciting the cooperation of the authorities of a State for the purpose of the investigation

SUMMONING AND QUESTIONING OF SUSPECTS
HEARING VICTIMS AND WITNESSES
GATHERING EVIDENCE
ON-SITE INVESTIGATION

Possibility of using a lower court judge to issue any orders required for the investigation

ACCUSED DISCHARGED
(end of case)

INITIATION OF PROSECUTION PROCEEDINGS

The Prosecutor draws up the bill of indictment

Delivery of the bill of indictment to a lower court judge for examination

ADJOURNMENT

REJECTION OF THE BILL OF INDICTMENT (end of case)

Observation: if there are new factors which might constitute additional proof, the Prosecutor may create a new bill of indictment

CONFIRMATION OF THE BILL OF INDICTMENT

Issue of the orders and mandates required for the conduct of the proceedings at the requisition of the Prosecutor.

Publication of the bill of indictment and its despatch to the States on whose territory the accused is likely to be found

Committal to one of the two lower courts = official indictment

OPENING OF LOWER COURT PROCEEDINGS

SUBMISSION OF THE EVIDENCE: Prosecution, evidence defence evidence, rejoinder from the Prosecutor, option of additional evidence being required by the lower court.
PLEADINGS: Prosecution address, response from the defence, reply by the Prosecutor, rejoinder by the defence.
DELIBERATION IN CAMERA: Guilty verdict by a majority of the panel of judges.

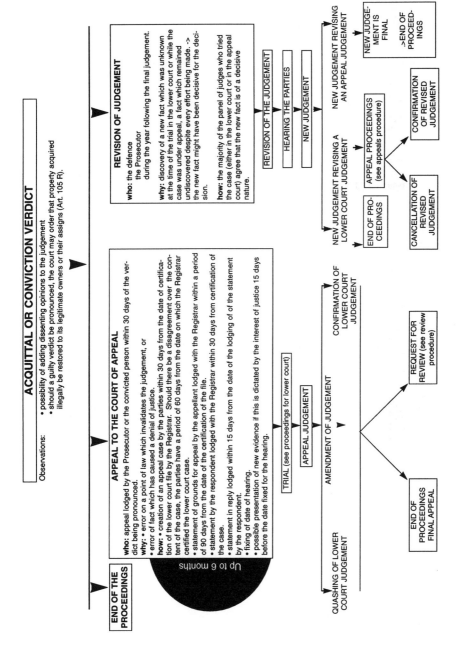

ACQUITTAL OR CONVICTION VERDICT

Observations:
- possibility of adding dissenting opinions to the judgement
- should a guilty verdict be pronounced, the court may order that property acquired illegally be restored to its legitimate owners or their assigns (Art. 105 R).

END OF THE PROCEEDINGS

APPEAL TO THE COURT OF APPEAL

who: appeal lodged by the Prosecutor or the convicted person within 30 days of the verdict being pronounced.

why: • error on a point of law which invalidates the judgement, or
• error of fact which has caused a denial of justice.

how: • creation of an appeal case by the parties within 30 days from the date of certification of the lower court file by the Registrar. Should there be a disagreement over the content of the case, the parties have a period of 60 days from the date on which the Registrar certified the lower court case.
• statement of grounds for appeal by the appellant lodged with the Registrar within a period of 90 days from the date of the certification of the file.
• statement in reply lodged within 15 days from the date of of the lodging of of the statement by the respondent lodged with the Registrar within 30 days from certification of the case.
• fixing of date of hearing.
• possible presentation of new evidence if this is dictated by the interest of justice 15 days before the date fixed for the hearing.

Up to 6 months

TRIAL (see proceedings for lower court)

APPEAL JUDGEMENT

AMENDMENT OF JUDGEMENT — CONFIRMATION OF LOWER COURT JUDGEMENT

QUASHING OF LOWER COURT JUDGEMENT

END OF PROCEEDINGS FINAL APPEAL

REQUEST FOR REVIEW (see review procedure)

REVISION OF JUDGEMENT

who: the defence
the Prosecutor
during the year following the final judgement.

why: discovery of a new fact which was unknown at the time of the trial in the lower court or while the case was under appeal, a fact which remained undiscovered despite every effort being made. -> the new fact might have been decisive for the decision.

how: the majority of the panel of judges who tried the case (either in the lower court or in the appeal court) agree that the new fact is of a decisive nature.

REVISION OF THE JUDGEMENT

HEARING THE PARTIES

NEW JUDGEMENT

NEW JUDGEMENT REVISING A LOWER COURT JUDGEMENT

NEW JUDGEMENT REVISING AN APPEAL JUDGEMENT

END OF PROCEEDINGS

APPEAL PROCEEDINGS (see appeals procedure)

CANCELLATION OF REVISED JUDGEMENT

CONFIRMATION OF REVISED JUDGEMENT

NEW JUDGEMENT IS FINAL

->END OF PROCEEDINGS

NIJHOFF LAW SPECIALS

1. D. Campbell: *Abortion Law and Public Policy.* 1984   ISBN 90-247-3107-0
2. J. Pictet: *Development and Principles of International Humanitarian Law.* 1985
     ISBN 90-247-3199-2
3. J. van Houtte: *Sociology of Law and Legal Anthropology in Dutch-speaking Countries.* 1985   ISBN 90-247-3175-5
4. C.D. De Fouloy: *Glossary of NAFTA Terms.* 1994   ISBN 0-7923-2719-5
5. H.L. Zielinski: *Health and Humanitarian Concerns.* Principles and Ethics. 1994
     ISBN 0-7923-2963-5
6. K.S. Foster and D.C. Alexander: *Prospects of a US-Chile Free Trade Agreement.* 1994   ISBN 0-7923-2885-X
7. F.J.M. Feldbrugge (ed.): *Russian Federation Legislative Survey. June 1990-December 1992.* 1995   ISBN 0-7923-3243-1
8. R. Platzöder (ed.): *The 1994 United Nations Convention on the Law of the Sea.* Basic Documents with an Introduction. 1995   ISBN 0-7923-3271-7
9. D. Warner (ed.): *New Dimensions of Peacekeeping.* 1995
     ISBN 0-7923-3301-2
10. M. van Leeuwen (ed.): *The Future of the International Nuclear Non-Proliferation Regime.* 1995   ISBN 0-7923-3433-7
11. E.-U. Petersmann: *International and European Trade and Environmental Law After the Uruguay Round.* 1995   ISBN 90-411-0857-2
12. V. Gowlland-Debbas: *The Problem of Refugees in the Light of Contemporary International Law Issues.* 1996   ISBN 90-411-0085-7
13. A. Kaczorowska: *International Trade Conventions and Their Effectiveness.* Present and Future. 1995   ISBN 0-7923-3362-4
14. T.F. Acuña: *The United Nations Mission in El Salvador.* A Humanitarian Law Perspective. 1995   ISBN 90-411-0123-3
15. H. Wiggering and A. Sandhövel (eds.): *European Environmental Advisory Councils.* 1996   ISBN 90-411-0873-4
16. E.A. Ankumah: *The African Commission on Human and Peoples' Rights.* Practice and Procedures. 1996   ISBN 90-411-0130-6
17. B. de Rossanet: *Peacemaking and Peacekeeping in Yugoslavia.* 1996
     ISBN 90-411-0192-6
18. A. Webster and K. Packer (eds.): *Innovation and the Intellectual Property System.* 1996   ISBN 90-411-0907-2
19. H. Bocken and D. Ryckbost (eds.): *Codification of Environmental Law.* Draft Decree on Environmental Policy. 1996   ISBN 90-411-0911-0
20. K. Lescure and F. Trintignac: *International Justice for Former Yugoslavia.* The Working of the International Criminal Tribunal of the Hague. 1996
     ISBN 90-411-0201-9

MARTINUS NIJHOFF PUBLISHERS – THE HAGUE / BOSTON / LONDON